Old West/New West

UNIVERSITY OF OKLAHOMA PRESS
NORMAN AND LONDON

Gene M Gressley, Editor

Old West/New West

Library of Congress Cataloging-in-Publication Data

Old west/new west / Gene M. Gressley, editor. — Oklahoma pbk. ed.
p. cm.
Includes index.
ISBN 0-8061-2962-X (pbk. : alk. paper)
1. West (U.S.)—Historiography. I. Gressley, Gene M., 1931– .
F591.0624 1997
978'.0072—dc21 97-9215
CIP

The paper in this book meets the guidelines for permanence and durability of the Committee on Production Guidelines for Book Longevity of the Council on Library Resources, Inc. ♾

"The Privileges and Perils of the Western Public Intellectual" by Patricia Nelson Limerick, first published in *Encyclia, The Journal of the Utah Academy of Sciences, Arts, and Letters* Volume 68, 1991, is used with permission.

An abbreviated version of "The New Western History" by Gerald Thompson was presented as an address at the Phi Alpha Theta luncheon, annual meeting of the Organization of American Historians, April 16, 1993. It was published in *Continuity,* 1993.

All drawings courtesy of the Hans Kleiber Collection, American Heritage Center, University of Wyoming.

Oklahoma Paperbacks edition published 1997 by the University of Oklahoma Press, Norman, Publishing Division of the University, by arrangement with High Plains Publishing Company, Inc., P.O. Box 1860, Worland, Wyoming 82401. Manufactured in the U.S.A. First printing of the University of Oklahoma Press edition, 1997.

1 2 3 4 5 6 7 8 9 10

For Earl Pomeroy
Who has bridged East and West
and the Old West/New West

Contents

GENE M. GRESSLEY

Prologue

On a soft summer evening in August of 1990, a book editor and five historians of the American West were savoring the culinary delights of Leo Goto's Wellshire Inn on South Colorado Boulevard in Denver. The discussion had became quite animated, focusing on a hot topic for the historians—the current historiography of the American West. All of a sudden, the book editor brought the conversation to a halt: "I have been listening to all of you for more than two hours, and I' m confused! Define for me precisely what you mean by 'Old West' and 'New West.'" Then he added with a mischievous chuckle, "In twenty-five words or less."

In response to that question and out of that evening sitting in a booth overlooking the Wellshire golf course in the summer twilight came this book. During the next year, I contacted the contributors asking for their interpretations and assessments of the history of the West.

As readers of this volume will discern, the contemporary state of western history is a boiling, roiling pot, as pungent as any chili issuing from "Maria's" restaurant in Santa Fe—an interpretive milieu that emerges from the template of the 1960s. The generation of the sixties, a decade that has become synonymous with rebellious, idealistic youth, was bent not only on challenging the "silent generation" of the fifties but also on staging a revolution against the world of their parents.

The style of the sixties was programmed by the affluent cream of its generation. Highly impressionable and susceptible to the clarion call to national service by a handsome, articulate, young president, the youth of the sixties enrolled in colleges in astonishing numbers. In 1960, college enrollment in the United States approximated four million; by 1970, that number had doubled. Increasingly these collegians became more and more alienated by what they perceived as the crimes of our society—nuclear testing, the violation of civil rights, the assassination of John F. Kennedy, and, above all, the war in Vietnam. Indeed, the escalation of the Vietnam War after 1965 polarized the New Left movement.

The leaders of the Students for a Democratic Society advocated political reform via a participatory democracy, which was ostensibly keyed to transforming American society along a broad front. Their platform was shattered by the killing of four protesting students at Kent State University. All of a sudden, students of the sixties realized that one could be killed just as easily on the rolling hills in a corner of northeast Ohio as in Vietnam. Reality soon conquered injustice. The antiwar activists, totally frustrated by their failure to gain the attention of the nation to terminate the war in Vietnam, gave up their dreams to bring about an American Spring, and turned their attention to other causes; particularly the environment, feminism, and the treatment of minorities (especially blacks, Chicanos, and Native Americans). These causes became the tenets in the creed of the New Western historians of the 1980s—historians who had been undergraduates in the 1960s.

Arising from the insurgency of the sixties, though sans the gestation of Phoenix, two parallel, interrelated crusades came to rest in the academy: though political correctness, PC, did not originate in a university setting, it flourished in the halls of ivy. Indeed, over the past thirty years political correctness has evolved through the several stages of social protest from feminism to deconstructionism. [1] Legions of PCers cling to one of the vibrant characteristics of their holy war—that of viewing all of society's ills in political terms. Some critics of the political correctness doctrine go so far as to maintain that not only do PCers perceive all intellectual problems as having a political dimension but that in universities, faculty decisions are molded via a political bias. As evidence these disenchanted point to curricula that are designed for no other rationale than to correct past injustices and to subscribe to minority positions.

Where did it all begin? Some commentators have ascribed roots to centuries-old Protestant theology. Depending on the polemicists you read and/or believe, George Orwell first warned modern man of the dangers of political correctness in his classic essay "Politics and the English Language," written almost a half-century ago.[2] The lineage descends next to Michel Foucault and particularly Herbert Marcuse and his famous polemic, "Repressive Tolerance." The phrase "political correctness" was popularized by the New Left, especially by the Black Panthers, who, according to some, originated it. The youth of the sixties and the seventies found refuge in this illiberal spirit and became increasingly alienated from the American political tradition.

The accusations of those who pose the PC position are as shrill as their opponents are that political correctness jihad is just another manifestation of McCarthyism, only this time in the dress of the New Left. To which the advocates of political correctness fire back at their attackers with a fusillade of contentions, including that their critics ridicule the PC stance before they understand it. Even worse than those who suffer from a lack of comprehension are detractors who employ the derisive tactic of making the PC posture ridiculous by relating a shocking example. The PCers favorite illustration is a Dinesh d'Souza anecdote about Frank Lentricchia, a professor of English at Duke, who showed the film *The Godfather* to dramatize the position that organized crime is a metaphor for American business as a whole. Never mind that Puzo had expressed this idea in his book—the tale, so PCers claim, is repeated with horrific effect in article after article.

Another retort of the PCers is that their message, admittedly ideological, is really very simplistic, if subtly sophisticated.

The bulletin is simply that ideological factors are playing the role of midwife in American culture—a raison d'être that has not been realized. Their critics contend that surely if this is all the PCers mean to say, they manage to bury their translation under layers of obtuse and foggy semantics embedded in debates of textual criticism, deconstruction, historicism, and other games of intellectual ping pong.

Then in a flash of inspiration, perhaps with the blinding realization that just possibly they may have lost their audience (presumably the voting everyman), that academicians may really only be talking to academicians, as Patricia Limerick has beautifully described (and even worse, English faculties only conversing with English faculties), PCers will, with histrionics, dramatize their point with a reference for the common man. Not that the deconstructed public always understands or always believes these derogatory propaganda bytes such as the antisemitism (a particularly antique ploy) of William Shakespeare, or the racial intolerance and ambiguity of William Faulkner. Whatever may be their condescending thoughts of reaching out to the readers in the arena of *Time*, *Newsweek*, or *Playboy*, the water in the hot tub of the political correctness controversy swirls around in academe.

The vigor, vitriol, and violence of the academic debate centers in literature departments, where presumably all are comfortable thriving on the morals of esoteric translations of deconstructionism and multiculturalism. Here in canon to the right and canon to the left, the victims, rather than the lowly aborigine, are their nontenured colleagues (when they have the courage to speak out, which understandably is not very frequently).

The armaments of the cultural wars then are targeted on the humanities—particularly the teaching of them. The traditionalists, perhaps best exemplified by the late Allan Bloom, Dinesh d'Souza, C. Vann Woodward, Roger Kimball, and George Will, defend the ramparts of what they perceive as the rituals of higher education.[3] As is common in pedagogical debates in general, these traditionalists are often foggy about the trenches they are defending. If pressed, they would announce their fervent belief in cadre of works issuing from the Greeks and the Romans in direct lineal descent to the present—which represents to them the western intellectual tradition. You are not an educated individual, so their logic goes, unless you have imbibed this rich, universal intellectual heritage.

The Socratic metaphysics has hardly escaped from the word processors of a Roger Kimball, a Hilton Kramer, or a George Will before they are challenged by a Sara Diamond, a Barbara Ehrenreich, or a Martin Duberman. These critics quickly shout, if you only casually peruse the synopticon of the Great Books you soon discover that they were almost all written by White European or North American males. A vast literature reflecting ethnic groups, women, and the Eastern world is ignored. The obvious rejoinder of the traditionalist should be, "Fine, let's enlarge the catalogue raisonné of Western literature to include the non-Western liturgy. Indeed, we will not exclude any significant literature that has contributed to world civilization."

Unfortunately, traditionalists and their New Left opponents seem to be more devoted to confrontation than to winning converts—until their battlements become so polarized as to thwart accommodation. The traditionalists insist that they have the divine word, that the multiculturalists have shunned quality. They then dig in their heels and maintain that material that is considered for inclusion in the traditionalist legacy must meet two criteria: merit and historical authority. Furthermore, the traditionalists claim the multiculturalists have sunk in a swamp of the parochial, where they dream of the provincial. Education via the multiculturalists, according to these dissenters, does not liberate the individual spirit but shackles that spirit to a narrow viewpoint with a macular perspective. If forced, the traditionalists also will concede to an elitist premise: The heritage of the West has more universalism—a unique philosophical worldliness, if you will, that denotes in the educational jargon of the 1930s—"maximizing the potential of the individual."

What perhaps irritates traditionalists most is that they discern a rampant relativism in the lore of the multiculturalists. How do you teach reality, when that reality keeps flashing, like a neon sign? Finally, the traditionalists point with pride to self-criticism as a percept of the Western intellectual tradition. From Socrates to Bertrand Russell, the travails of Western civilization have been proclaimed again and again through the rite of withering self-criticism.

Undeniably and unequivocally, in one major sense, the multiculturalists have the final salute in the debate. Like it or not, America's future will be multicultural. The world is shrinking, the population of America is darkening. In 1960, ninety-five percent of the college students were white. In 1990, twenty percent were non-white. In 1960 forty percent of college students were female; in 1990 that figure had risen to fifty-five percent. A monochromatic horizon is not in the future of America's populace.

In further opposition to the traditionalists, the multiculturalists frequently present the flip side of the traditionalist logic. Rather than shun or disguise your ethnic past, you should be proud of it and realize that this very background identifies and defines you. In addition, no rationalization is necessary to realize that the cosmic view of the traditionalists is simply self-deception—gender, race, and class are the most important characteristics for an educational process.

Sanctifying the Western heritage, claim the multiculturalists, is not only elitist but downright snobbish. Though the multiculturalists may waffle before admitting it, they really appear to be saying that all cultures are equal. Diversity then becomes the buzz word—diversity of curriculum, students, and faculty.

Closely associated with the political metaphysics of the multiculturalists is their notion of empowerment. Their syllogism maintains that status and power in the United States are held by white males; therefore, white males are culturally dominant. The next step is a foregone conclusion—minorities, especially females (though one could argue their "minority" status) are disenfranchised politically and exploited culturally.

Wherever one falls on the traditionalist-multiculturalist spectrum, unless one understands that the politicization of the university is at issue, much of the point and counterpoint of the debate lacks relevance. Though the multiculturalists vehemently protest the deduction as WASP propaganda, it is difficult to escape the inference that achievement must be judged on the basis of ethnicity and gender rather than merit.

All of which leads to a, if not the, linchpin in the multiculturalist argument: the victim as hero. Victimization is seen everywhere in American society and culture. The redemption for our cultural sins will only come about through a total re-ordering of the social-cultural staircase. In this orthodoxy, the noble savage and the pioneer woman become the exploited and downtrodden—THE VICTIMS. For the multiculturalist the cultural wars are not only necessary; they are inevitable. How else can we exculpate our shame except by the spectacle of profuse and abject apology revealed through cultural redemption? The problem, of course, is readily expanded in the facade of expressionism—culture becomes the passing parade. Many multiculturalists will hoot at such an inference as simply a traditional parody of pluralism. Further, they argue that such a thesis confuses the tribalism of political correctness with multiculturalism.

Multiculturalists are correct to the extent that considerable histrionics in the hysteria of the cultural wars must be admitted. The canon, whether pronounced by traditionalists or multiculturalists, is conveyed as immutable, polarized, and inflexible. Removing the intolerance of the embittered of both sides should be a major effort of our educational docket for the coming future. For instance, a quick glance at the remedial offerings in college catalogs confirms the impression of illiteracy—and not just of a cultural bias.

Standards are being eroded by a know-nothing attitude, enhanced by the current university campaigns of "retention and recruitment equals economic salvation." So you have administrative tactical pressure for grade inflation and a dilution of subject matter.

As Todd Gitlin has observed, we live in a sound-byte culture that "has taken anti-elitism as a sacred principle."

Many multiculturalists also believe that to be simply defined as a Hispanic, a black, a female is justification enough for one's existence and identity. Are differences so crucial that they have erased the possibility of seeing any commonality? Further, one cannot dispute, with any credence, that the academy has become increasingly conformist. Long before multiculturalism was a campus byword, academe had suffered from an anti-intellectual conservatism. One fact of multiculturalism is not open to dispute. The complexion of the educational enrollment, reflecting our society, is losing its paleness. Diversity is not only inevitable but an empowerment to be reckoned with. The multicultural ideal is worth striving for, but it is an ideal that must be permeated with respect for an understanding of others. As ironic and as hackneyed as that statement is, some multiculturalists flaunt it by their deification of unqualified pluralism.

To this bubbling bouillabaisse of political correctness, multiculturalism, and New Left protest came a parade of historians who dumped into the pot an ingredient they termed the "new" social history.[4] Once again we behold the historians' obsession with the "cant of newness." In the past three decades we have witnessed the "new" political history, the "new" economic history, the "new" labor history—all of which were divorced from past methodology and interpretation, especially the consensus school. For in an era of tensions, conflict, and upheaval the consensus vision of national progress, cultural and intellectual accommodation to a peaceful history, appeared threadbare and sadly out of fashion.

Something "new" in intellectual gamesmanship was definitely in order. Sans ringing manifestos or blaring proclamations, articles on methodology and convention gossip began to pivot on the "new" social historians. What were they saying? First, in common with many new, if not fresh, intellectual diversions, the pitch was far from perfect. It was easier to describe what the new social history was not, than what it was. Most practicing and nonpracticing social historians quickly agreed that the hoary definition of the late G. M. Trevelyan ("The history of a people with politics left out") was a vacuous definition. Nor was it a catalog of social mores, daily living patterns, and material welfare as served up by Arthur M. Schlesinger, Sr., and Dixon Ryan Fox in their thirteen volume *History of American Life.* Above all, heaven forfend, there was no room for the consensus interpretation of the past.

The new social history came close in tone and historical roots to the French "Annales" school with its emphasis on short- and long-term historical "waves," underlying trends in civilization—especially climatology, economic trade, and geographic influences. The Annalists reached for the amorphous, and not always satisfying, "totality" of history. The additional legacy that the Annalists bequeathed to the new social history was their methodology with its emphasis on quantitative and sharp detail. Onto the Annales research techniques the new social historians grafted the approach of the behavioral scientists. A Marxist tinge, though often enthusiastically discounted as nonexistent, flowed through some of the new social history historiography.

As article after article and book after book was published under the banner of the new social history some of its major tenets became identifiable. Historians should be vigilant in utilizing narrative sources (invariably produced by a narrow elite). Historians' research techniques should be rigorous, especially in selecting quantitative data. Illustrative facts should always represent the mass of data from whence it was extracted. Historians should be careful that their search for revelation in detail does not mesmerize them into meaningless fragmentation. Finally, historians were urged in their exploration of a broad synthesis to cavort in the subfields of women's history, ethnic history, labor history, and social mobility.

Although the subfield fragmentation of the new social history frightened some of the field's most devoted practitioners, others sensed that the field had lost its direction. Nevertheless, these feelings of insecurity aside, numerous new social history partisans offered their curative and creative prescriptions. Thomas Bender aimed to "reconceptualize" the field via a broad interaction of the political and social process. Bender advocated that social historians should speak directly to the general public, with clear and forceful interpretations of how our nation had evolved and functioned. Bender's public culture avenue would leap beyond specialization and fragmentation—relating to the historical process to the populace in a way that had been missing since the era of the Progressive historians—Charles Beard, Frederick Jackson Turner, and Vernon Parrington.

Robert Berkhofer has joined Thomas Bender in observing that social historians of the contemporary scene should address the same topics—social democracy and class conflict—that so appealed to the Progressive historians. The Genoveses moved the social materialist interpretation into the arena of class conflict. The issue of class then became the axis from which to relate to race and gender. Unlike the Genoveses, Lawrence Veysey found the "central message" in the assertion of "representativeness of evidence." If social historians had achieved nothing else, wrote Veysey, their insight and insistence that the validity of quantitative data depended on how representative it was constituted a major advance in historiographical interpretation.

Against this tumultuous panorama of sixties dissent, political correctness, multiculturalism, and social history, the New Western History cracked its shell and wobbled into being. How to define the New Western History?[5] First and foremost, the revisionists, with unabashed ardor, assailed the lively ghost of Frederick Jackson Turner and his frontier thesis. Seemingly oblivious to fifty years of criticism of Turner, the New West historians began trashing Turner with unrefined virulence. Among Turner's greatest sins was his ethnocentricism and his concept of the frontier and free land as a breeding ground for American democracy. Turner was not only inaccurate, but worse—his prose had been so seductive as to ensnare and freeze the interpretive minds and mien of generations of western historians. Turner's triumphal tone of western settlement outraged the New West historians who contended that there was nothing glorious at all about enslaving Native Americans. The westering process that Turner described was not a heroic story at all, but rather a tale of greed, debasement, and exploitation. Failure, not success, was the guidon of the New Western History in depicting western settlement.

The West of Frederick Jackson Turner had been a West of progress, full of rugged individualism that melded with a democratic spirit, which in turn flowed along with civilization across a hostile land. The New West historians are much more concerned with continuity between East and West—especially from an economic viewpoint. They emphasize, as indeed did some of Turner's followers, that the West's resources and colonial status subsidized much of the West and much of the East's economy. Again, rapaciousness and greed were the keys to understanding the eastern onslaught of western settlement.

Critics of the New West's invention complained that emphasis on failure, hatred, and greed missed a higher plane of attainment in western colonization. The dreams inspired by "seeing the elephant" fever were real, not fictitious. The West of victimization, say these critics, was just as unreal as the romanticized West of Turner's heroic conquest. Further perturbing to the anti–New West detractors is the concept of the West as the land of victimization. They believe the New West historians are painting a West of confined regionalism, narrow provincialism, and myopic parochialism. Ideology, as Gerald Nash has written, was the driving force behind the vision of the New West historians.

The presentist orientation of New West historiography often results in superficial research. The absence of archival research is most pronounced. In common with much of the New Left historiography of two decades ago, New West historians go for the gold in the grand sweep: the breathtaking generality and the seductive syllogism. This methodology is all the more paradoxical when much in-depth research is essential if we are to detect even the surface structure of western history. The cosmetic West of the New West historiography then matches the journalistic style described by one of their critics as "gloom, doom and disaster all around." Realism has been achieved with a splash of funeral black. One can wonder whether the themes of the New West historiography will be around in a century to receive the broadside fusillade currently being leveled at Frederick Jackson Turner.

What appears to have disturbed the critics of the New Western history most was the heavy atmosphere of relativism that enveloped most of the New West historians' arguments. The New West historians, so their critics maintained, were enraptured by the prose of Paul de Man. [6] Even worse, the New West historians adopted some of the spirit and much of the message of the New Criticism of the literary world fostered by R. P. Blackmur—a criticism that had shed the historical and biographical past for the excitement of reading poems and novels sans background.

It was then only a short leap, according to the New West deprecators, from the New Criticism of Cleanth Brooks and Robert Penn Warren to the deconstructionist sermons of Paul de Man. Now the "text" became the be-all and end-all—authors were embalmed in textual criticism of the deconstructionists.

The politicization, the deconstructionism, and the relativism of the New History tormented many. One of the most eloquent and slashing attacks originated with art critic Robert Hughes. In *The New York Review of Books*, Hughes related, with feelings of confusion, his reaction to the show "The West as America" at the Smithsonian National Museum of American Art.[7] After suggesting that it was an "interesting," even a "stimulating," show, Hughes confessed what vexed him most was the catalog and particularly the wall labels. Noting that the inscriptions were suffused with Marxist and feminist diatribes, Hughes found the indoctrination and propaganda simply ridiculous. "Here folks is a picture of a Huron. Lo, the poor Native Americans! See he is depicted as dying." Hughes wrote, "A little of this goes a long way, and 'The West as America' had a lot of it." What astonished Hughes even more than the amateur propagandizing of the show was the virulent reaction by some of the members of Congress and conservative scholars and pundits, such as Daniel Boorstin. Why, he wondered, all the vehemence? Didn't these vilifiers realize that the West as legend had been under attack for years by social historians? In fact, Hughes argued that the show was neither unprecedented nor particularly original. So why all the fuss?

The answer, which Hughes would have conceded, was obvious. When you politicize the past, serving up history as propaganda—whether it is a John Wayne West or the West of the exploited, lowly aborigine—you no longer serve Clio but Lucifer.

The New West historians insisted that in their zeal to expose western myths and the self-serving quality of the white conquerors, they may have exaggerated in "The West as America Show." However, they pointed out, the tidings were far more accurate and responsible than the cinematic West—a West that never was.

Yet even the West of John Wayne is being transformed into the West of Clint Eastwood.[8] Perhaps the epitome as well as epitomizing the moral confusion of the "new" western came in 1992 with Clint Eastwood's *Unforgiven*. No shot is fired in Big Whiskey, Wyoming, until the Schofield Kid comes close to nervous prostration gunning down his amour in an unusual setting.

The new western, in a mirror of the New West historiography, demythologizes the West. *The Lonesome Dove* is crammed with the tedium, the grittiness, the drudgery of the cowboy—a West that was fantasized in the movies starring Roy Rogers and Gene Autry. The grubbier, politically correct, multicultural western evokes a West that saw the democratic spirit trampled, the environment ruined, and the aborigine toyed with in a brutal vanquishment. The *High Noon* cinematic West as a moral allegory has been redefined—once again. Not all the parable is lost; we still see a script of simple solutions—where nobility triumphs over low life. Today the evil and good are transposed, the sermon is more complex, more ambiguous. The scenery is as grand—indeed, even more dramatic courtesy of technological advances in optics.

One of the more arresting of the new westerns is *Geronimo*, in which director and writer Walter Hill builds on the periphery western of the past as embodied in the work of John Ford, Delmer Daves, and Sam Peckinpah. Daves could and did often produce the popcorn western of Saturday matinees, along with *Broken Arrow* (1950)—one of the first distinctly pro-Indian westerns.

What makes *Geronimo* a fascinating two hours is the docudrama quality of Hill's realism. Indians are not all saints, nor all devils. Unlike the director of *Dances With Wolves*, who portrays the Indian community as idyllic to the point of being maudlin (and the frontier army racist), Hill tells a lyrical story with pronounced understatement and craftsmanship. Although the outcome is never in doubt (Geronimo will be finally run down in the quixotic campaign), Hill never misses an opportunity to reveal, starkly and silently, the fact that a misguided Indian policy and injustice are the real miscreants. It is then all the sadder to realize that the tepid response, both critically and at the box office, probably foretells the doom of this realistic Walter Hill western.

The great unwashed will go along with a recasting and a redefinition of their mythology of the West, but they insist that morality come as all-dark or all-white. Evil does not appear in ghost-like shades of gray. In this vital sense, today's *Unforgiven, Tombstone, Lonesome Dove,* and *Dances With Wolves* are the flip side of yesterday's *Fort Apache, She Wore a Yellow Ribbon,* and *Rio Grande.* The complexities and the ambiguities of the western are sifted out for the 1994 audience that looks for and sees right triumphant over wrong—regardless of the intricacies of characterization.

Even if the New West historians did not always discover their message in the medium of current cinema and television, there was much that appealed to their orthodoxy. There can be little dispute with the fact that the role of women and minorities, if not ignored, at least was minimalized to the point of vacuousness in the 1935 western. The sidewalks of Denver in yesterday's western were often slighted for the boardwalks of Durango. The urban scene and its history were a backdrop for a more interesting and seemingly perpetual rural west.

Yet, as Carl Abbott and William Cronon have shown, there is a fascinating, yea, intricate tale told of the complex interaction between rural and urban affairs. The twentieth century, if not totally neglected (as the works of Earl Pomeroy and Gerald Nash have amply demonstrated), had, comparatively speaking, been slighted. The environment, except as a place for natural resource extraction or scenic attraction, had been neglected at best. The balance between environmentalists, developers, and ecologists is not only delicate and tender, but, as Donald Worster has evinced, must be resolved if that undefinable quality of life is to be more than an approximation of our dreams. The New Western historians' emphasis on regionalism, while not as "new" as they wish others to believe, has merit. And finally, yes, as many historians for several decades past have conceded, Frederick Jackson Turner did oversell his version of the westward movement.

So the New West historians have brought us into a presentist West, not on horseback but on the backs of coolie labor on the Union Pacific. What of the West of the 1990s? The popular press of the past five years has offered a mixture of upbeat messianic prophecy; "Boom in the Rockies," and "The Last Frontier" foretell environmental disaster and the vanishing of the good life style—unless we mend our evil ways. [9] True, the urban cowboys and endowed ranchers are sharing their tax-sheltered wealth via growing up with the country, so to speak. The Ralph Lauren good life ostensibly means moving West to enjoy all outdoors, leaving behind urban congestion and wearing western attire designed on Seventh Avenue!

But who owns or thinks they own the West is a persistent question. The answers come fast, if distorted by frozen opinion. The conservationists argue that the West should be held in trust for the nation—west, east, north, and south. No one owns our West.

The Endangered Species Act and the National Environmental Policy Act provide a federal foundation for the stance of conservation and ecology. The economic triad of ranching, mining, and timber that symbolized the West for a century is under a broad frontal attack. The grazing issue has become a vocal vortex of confrontation.

The livestock industry contends that the cost of public grazing fees disregards their investment in roads, fences, and water that only the private sector provides. The critics of the livestock industry say the ranchers pollute the streams, overgraze, and denude the domain. For all the antagonism between ranchers and environmentalists, these two groups will on occasion find common cause against a common enemy. Such an instance occurred more than two decades ago, when the boot-clad cowboys found themselves in the same town hall meeting with a sea of backpacking advocates of the wilderness. Who were they fighting? The enemy at that moment was the coal developer of the northern Great Plains.

The mining industry faces a major revision of the 1872 Mining Law—an artifice, critics claim, allowing the mining industry to become "The biggest scam still going on in America." Nothing so dramatizes the mining country, politically and economically, as the Carlin gold deposit in Nevada. An enormous, low-grade gold landscape is being chewed up by mega shovels, which tear up tons of earth, then drench the earth with cyanide in an extractive process described as heap leaching. Nothing so jump-starts the adrenalin as the sight of open-pit mines. The Sierra Club and Friends of the Earth spokesmen speak in the voices of doomsday—the miners are poisoning the land and the water, carving up the land into huge, gaping surfaced canyons and in general destroying the western scape for centuries. Mining companies, who have put in place large conservation departments to reclaim the domain, scoff at such jeremiad pronouncements. The mining entrepreneurs insist that with their assistance the fauna and flora will regenerate the land and that the devastation foreseen by the conservationist is merely a figment of the evangelist.

Though the environmentalist vents his spleen on miners refiguring the landscape, few environmentalist brawls rival the wilderness battles. Here profit motive and conservationist are in stark relief. The Wilderness Society maintains that the Forest Service subsidizes the lumber industry for road construction and administrative costs to the tune of $300 million plus per year. Loggers, fearful that acre upon acre of forest will be banned from production, see their personal futures as bartenders and motel managers. One of the most dramatic controversies was the federal program to protect the habitats of the spotted owl by restricting the harvest of old-growth forest in the Pacific Northwest.

Loggers, miners, and ranchers may be characters in the vanishing scenario of the West that was, but nothing so defines and divides the West as water. The hoary cliché that water is the life-blood of the West is not less true because it is a cliché. As Walter Prescott Webb reminded us more than a half century ago, water is the basis of civilization in the American West. Courthouses in the West have their dockets crammed with litigation pitting urban against rural, Native Americans against white (and all others), and government entity (state and/or federal) against governmental entity. The West is running out of water, the victim of the exploitation of its aquifers and the evaporation and nonrenewal of its rivers.

Dreams then are being downsized in the West, each western constituency striving to protect its way of life before its resource base is exhausted. The decade of the 1980s saw employment growth in the West center almost entirely on light manufacturing, and the service—specifically tourism and recreation—industries.

A new high-tech boom ushered in by the fax, the modem, and the computer have liberated these gurus from "place." These "lone eagles," as Phil Burgess, director of the Center for the New West, describes them, have moved from Wall Street to Jackson, Wyoming, and Aspen, Colorado. Reveling in a quality of life of mountain valleys, bugling elk, wild flowers, and million-dollar abodes, they wonder why they slaved for so many years on Battery Lane. They indulge themselves in luxurious living—where luxury itself comes in many fashions.

This then is the West of the vagabonding affluent but not, others claim, the "true" West of rancher, miner, and logger. Nor is it the modern West with its underclass of restaurant employees, motel maids, and clerks at discount merchandisers. The booming West of the service economy produces four-hour daily commuters because of the divorcement of affordable housing and employment. In this script, the Chevy hobo from Victor, Idaho, to Jackson Hole finds a kinship with the Long Island commuter from Darien to Manhattan—the scenery is vastly more beautiful but the exploitation of time and money is comparable. The service-supported West is the non-existent, nondescribed West of travel brochures and real estate ads. The modern West is a West of half-tones.

The West of political correctness, of multiculturalism, cyclical economy, of generational dissent (past and present) and minority rebellion has become the West of the New Left. The West, as the following chapters will amplify, is obviously not the West of many historians or their audiences. The more traditional historians, if you will, shun the postmodernist intellectual vogue of anthropological and literary ideological gymnastics. These historians with less relativism in their intellectual baggage find little stimulation in the intellectual sport of their politically correct colleagues.

The New West historians have not moved on to the field of Agincourt with superior intellectual weapons, but they have demonstrated an impressive array of youthful enthusiasm and energy—and some might even say fanaticism. And although the New West agenda is often neither new nor original, the emphasis has been adopted by those who run from deconstruction but concede that the topics of the underside West, the environmental West, and the urban West bear examination.

No single individual is more identified with the canon of the New Western history than Patricia Nelson Limerick of the University of Colorado. Her countenance and byline have been splashed across the pages of *USA Today*, *Newsweek*, and the *American Historical Review*, to name a few publications. Effervescent, spontaneous, and evangelistic, possessed of a writing style many journalists envy, Professor Limerick burst upon the stage of western history with a book, *The Legacy of Conquest: The Unbroken Past of the American West*—which was the quintessence of the New Western History. With passionate prose and missionary zeal, Professor Limerick proceeded to turn western history upside down: Where there had been conquerors, there were now victims; where there were triumphs, now there were defeats; where there had been the West of the white settler, there was now the west of minorities—black, Hispanic, women, and the Native Americans.

In her chapter, Patricia Limerick discusses a subject dear to her personal theology; she speculates on the "privileges and the perils" of being a public intellectual in the West. She finds the intellectual of the campus West "privatized," cowering in dark corners of academe, writing unreadable prose for an audience in absentia. Insecure, inarticulate, isolated, and entrapped in outmoded theories, the western public intellectual is in worse shape than the oil-drenched condor. What is her remedy for this lost species, this mutant spirit? Professor Limerick serves up an eight-point program to revitalize and reenergize the scene of the western intellectuals. The reformation of these "new" intellectuals will come about if they first go to confession; they must request absolution for the error of their ways; they are challenged to take the broad-jump leap of synthesizer; productive they must be but also intense and civil in debate. These "new" intellectuals avoid specialization and narrowness; they flee academic jargon with the realization that to employ same means the loss of audience; these new intellectuals keep their wits about them with grace and humor; they must be willing to engage in communication via correspondence with the great sea of the general public; and finally new western intellectuals are willing to learn this presumably savant exchange. This article, as all her admirers and detractors will quickly recognize, is vintage Limerick.

Professor Gerald Thompson of the University of Toledo has taken to heart some of the healing prescriptions of Patricia Limerick's sick intellectual. In broad, sweeping, and impressive synthesis, Gerald Thompson finds much to applaud in the New Western history, such as the emphasis on the twentieth century, the burnished image of women, and the prominence given the environment and the continuity between nineteenth and twentieth centuries.

Thompson observes that the New West historians pursued their research of specialty rather than unfolding an extensive framework. In this proclivity, the New West historians were stepping in tune with the new social historians.

More and more, "native westerners" initiated discussions of their theses by employing the concept of region, although they commonly had trouble deciding what the parameters of a region were. To the question "Is there a New West history?" Thompson answers with a resounding "Yes." He emphasizes, though, the historiography of the New West heritage is long and deep, encompassing far more than the outpourings of those historians whose work appeared in the 1980s.

But Thompson also detects much that disturbs in the Holy Writ of the New Western History, especially the negativism and the presentism. He then asks, "Has the New West historian really generated a substantive interpretive framework that replaces Frederick Jackson Turner's frontier thesis?" Professor Thompson is not convinced that the New West scripture has given us the Holy City: perhaps it's only a western Babylon.

One of the New West preoccupations that builds on the work of Gerald Nash and Earl Pomeroy is the urbanization of the West. Professor Carl Abbott, in his provocative chapter, unfolds the urban revolution and development. The urban west, as John Findlay notes, was far more organized and thematic than is usually conceded. Carl Abbott's model for Findlay's magic kingdoms comes replete with a comparative approach and modernization. The modern movement for these urbanites meant adopting new technologies and living socially and culturally diverse lives. Though the hinterlands were isolated longer than is usually realized, Abbott deduces that the termination of mercantile capitalism transformed the entire West. The urban entrepreneur connected the West directly to regional (Donald Worster's "third way of being American"), national, and global markets; the globalization of the West was dramatized by the economic penetration of the Pacific Rim.

While Carl Abbott's West is one of mercantile dynamics, Professor Donald Worster of the University of Kansas finds his West in the environment. Writing in a seductive, eloquent prose, Donald Worster has long been captivated by the problem of aridity. In two prize-winning and much discussed books, *Dust Bowl: The Southern Plains in the 1930s* (1979) and *Rivers of Empire: Water, Aridity and the Growth of the American West* (1986), Worster excavated his Kuhn-like paradigm.

For Worster the land is the West. Worster proceeds to delineate a John Wesley Powell who has been lost not only to the West but to history. The Powell that Worster uncovers is far more radical than the Powell of previous biographers; Worster reveals a Powell whose social order would environ a region of small irrigated farms and ranches. A rural populace inhabits a region "bound together in a common body politic." Fractured, independent and possessive, the whites in contrast to Indians and Hispanics, failed to understand the interrelationship of their lives, their land, and their neighbors. "That in a nutshell," writes Worster, "was the central ecological problem of the West." Powell, more ignored than scorned, could not sell his vision of the West.

Local control was fine, but the collective nature of Powell's recommendations bothered the nineteenth-century settler committed to a philosophy of the land lying open for the taking. Economic progress and environmental accommodation were incompatible, if even considered, in the minds of those who fanned west across the 100th meridian.

In conclusion, Donald Worster lays out an ambitious precis for historians of the West. After saying that his "ambition for western history" is to see a complete environmental history written, Worster informs his readers that that means a story of every one of the hydrographic regions that Powell envisioned. Second, he hopes to eventually read the environmental history of every group of westerners whether they be Basques, Oriental, or Hispanics. Third, Worster would like to have a history of all species of fauna and flora in the West. This daunting assignment is enough to keep several generations of western historians occupied for their lifetimes.

While Donald Worster is concerned with the operational mode of the western immigrant, Malcolm Rohrbough, in a penetrating and insightful chapter, examines the ideology of these newcomers in his "First American West," circa 1790-1850, and "Second American West," 1850 to present. Rohrbough seeks to understand the credo of Worster's rapacious exploiters on their way West. The western migrants, Professor Rohrbough reminds us, almost immediately exhibited two characteristics that they carried with them as part and parcel of their intellectual baggage. Local in orientation, these settlers west were imbued with popular sovereignty. Second, from the instant they plunged into the forest they flaunted their exploitation of natural resources. These two characteristics flowed in a continuum through successive generations that struggled through time and geography. A third ideological stool that these immigrants brought with them was a blending of the spirit of manifest destiny with national interest. A fourth characteristic of this not-so-new character—the westerner—was an ambivalence toward the federal government. Damning the government with pyrotechnic rhetoric, the westerners would with unseeming rapidity reach out their hands to Washington for an outpouring of federal largesse in the form of public works and subsidies.

Professor Rohrbough perceives the direction of the New West historians as beneficial, particularly their stress on the interaction of cultures, the continuity between nineteenth and twentieth centuries, the cooperation and, yes, the competition between inhabitants. Rohrbough's reconnaissance of the future for historians of the West is limitless. He writes, "No other field offers such a wide range of peoples, times, places, and cultures."

While Malcolm Rohrbough confronts the morrow of western history with optimism, Professor Gerald Nash in an erudite, pro-vocative, and free-ranging essay warns of the inherent dangers of the New West design. Cast against the global world, Nash quickly acknowledges the presentism-relativism value that can be derived by each age reappraising its past. Nash suggests that such a reevaluation may not only be stimulating but refreshing.

Professor Nash emphasizes that the historiography of the New West is not "necessarily of a totalitarian bent"; further that it is his desire to place the New West historians "in a historical context, rather than castigate them in one way or another." Professor Nash then cautions us that there are similar ideological embryos between the New West and authoritarianism, fertilized in centuries past, in the seedbed of Prussian nationalism, Stalinist Russia, Japanese militarism, and the New Left. The New Left and the Right trumpet the fox and the hedgerow of negativism, class stereotypical victims, moral righteousness, paranoia, intolerance, and confined cultural outlook. It is this nihilism, the one-dimensional underside view of western history, that disturbs Gerald Nash—a weltanschauung of moral rectitude, which has been played out on a world stage in century after century, a drama that pronounces its own warning to all but the nonhearing and the insensitive. It is to this heavy hand of the past that Gerald Nash wants historians of the West to be attuned.

In any intellectual exercise of this nature the debts are many, the acknowledgments all too brief. To Dr. Lawrence M. Woods who underwrote the project—our appreciation; to Joyce, who has been present on every page for some forty-two years—my gratitude.

Gene M. Gressley
Laramie, Wyoming
clear, blustery, 34
March 11, 1994

PATRICIA NELSON LIMERICK

The Privileges and Perils of the Western Public Intellectual

At first glance, the public intellectual resembles the California condor. In earlier ages, there were plenty of condors, and plenty of public intellectuals. Condors had plenty of places to nest, and plenty of flying opportunities, and plenty of things to eat; public intellectuals had plenty of places to speak, and plenty of publishing opportunities, and plenty of things to say. And then, both the condors and the public intellectuals fell on hard times, and their numbers dropped to where their friends and admirers feared that they would disappear entirely. But here we come to the principal difference between the condor and the public intellectual—the condors began to disappear because of outside forces, and the public intellectuals began to disappear, primarily, by their own choice. For the condors, the climate changed, the terrain and the ground cover changed, DDT and other strange new challenges to the physiological system entered the picture; but the public intellectuals, on their own, packed up and retreated to the refuge of colleges and universities.

Some might dispute my explanation here. Some might say that there *were* outside forces working against the intellectuals—television and mass media in general, and a decline of interest in and respect for serious mental activity. But this is still the fact: the intellectuals retreated, of their own will; they left the battlefield before the battle really started; they took one look at the enemy and said, "That's it; we've lost; we can't fight television." The condors, by contrast, facing enemies considerably more fearful than television, showed a little more spunk, with a few birds continuing to hold on to what they still had in the way of ecological niches. Professors, though, retreated to the university, and, just in case the public tried to follow them there, they defended their turf with barricades of dull, difficult, unreadable prose, with sentences whose tangled phrases and clauses formed a literary equivalent of barbed wire, with jargonized, polysyllabic sentences functioning as so many "Keep Out; No Trespassing" signs for the public. And so public intellectuals became an endangered species, and academics, what we might call private intellectuals, became ever more numerous, and talked to each other, and wrote for each other, and the public lost a vital part of its navigational system.

Heaven knows there are exceptions to this pattern. One could make a particularly good case for the viability of the Utah-shaped or Utah-based public intellectual—Wallace Stegner and Bernard DeVoto, or Leonard Arrington, Juanita Brooks, and Sterling McMurrin. In Utah, and elsewhere, there are professors who refused to join in the general retreat, and there are organizations like the State Endowment for the Humanities, of which Utah has a particularly successful version, that continued to lure academics out of their bunkers and burrows and into a dialogue with the public. But I stand by the accuracy of this general pattern—like condors, public intellectuals became an endangered species; and unlike condors, public intellectuals did this in a matter of a few decades, instead of a few centuries or millennia.

But that is also the good news—if the withdrawal took place so recently, and so fast, then a return could take place with equal speed and efficiency. The universities and colleges could suddenly open their doors, and, in a scene like the start of a football game, the intellectuals could suddenly stream out of the tunnel, onto the field, a revived and energized team, ready to give television a run for its money. It is a handsome vision, especially if the intellectuals could adopt one ritual from the University of Colorado football team and borrow our mascot, the buffalo Ralphie, to lead them as they run energetically onto the playing field. I want the buffalo there because I want to accent the regional element of my hopes: that the re-emergence of the public intellectual is occurring first in the American West.

How that happened, *why* that happened, is what I would like to address now, but first I want to tell a story that shows the start of affairs seven or eight years ago, when the changes that I am talking about today were just beginning. I had just moved to Boulder in 1984; I had been there maybe forty-eight hours when my chair called to tell me that one of my new colleagues had lost a bet and, as the price of losing, had to treat us all to a celebration. That seemed a festive way to be welcomed to Colorado—until, in the midst of the festivities, I asked what the occasion was. What bet had my colleague made and lost? He had bet, it seems, that I would default on my commitment to move to Boulder, that I would accept the job and then stand them up. This news had the effect of reducing the cheerfulness of the occasion, but I pressed ahead and asked the follow-up question: why had this man thought that I was inclined to default on my promises? It wasn't that, he said; it was that he couldn't see why anyone would leave the East Coast to move to Colorado.

It was at that moment that I detected a morale problem among Western intellectuals. The "I wouldn't join any club that would have me for a member" syndrome has a pretty deep root system in the American West. Why? The reasons are, to put it mildly, arbitrary. The Puritans went to New England, and not to Oregon; Harvard was founded in Massachusetts, and not in New Mexico; Thomas Jefferson lived in Virginia, and not in Kansas. Whatever the reasons, Westerners have long had the habit of believing that historical significance and intellectual sophistication have traditionally grown weak and frail when they get more than fifty miles from the Atlantic Coast. If, on the occasion of my welcome to Boulder, I initially felt bad because of the apparent insult to *my* honor, I ended up feeling more resentful on the insult to the West's honor.

A lot has happened since 1984, and by one curious chain of events, the burden of having to apologize for being in the West, of yearning to be somewhere more sophisticated and significant, has lifted considerably. Since this is a case study in the re-emergence of public intellectuals, and since it is the only such case study I know firsthand, I will take the liberty of telling the story of this curious chain of events.

In 1988, the state councils or endowments for the humanities in Arizona, Colorado, New Mexico, Utah, and Wyoming agreed to form a larger unit called the Rocky Mountain Resource Network and to undertake a joint project. They did a twenty-four-panel traveling exhibit called "Trails Through Time," on the routes of convergence of diverse people in the Rocky Mountain region, and I became the principal scholar for the exhibit. As a part of our grant proposal to the National Endowment for the Humanities, we could include a proposal for a symposium to launch the exhibit. "Did we want the symposium to be on trails?" the humanities people asked me. Well, no, I was already anticipating a great sense of overexposure to the topic of trails. After a summer devoted entirely to reading, writing, thinking, dreaming about Trails, I did not think that I wanted to celebrate the completion of the project with two-and-a-half days of speeches about trails. But we had to use the word in the symposium conference, and so I suggested we call it "Trails: Toward a New Western History," and the speakers would address, directly, how much had changed in the writing of Western History in the last twenty years.

Then, as the time of the symposium approached, I began to get restive with the word "toward." Western American historians had done a great deal of "calling" for new models and new approaches. With this "toward" business, I began to fear that I would be convening us all in Santa Fe for two days of more calling for, more hoping for, more yearning for new models and new approaches. So I wrote the participants and asked them to drop the word "toward." Let us go to this conference in Santa Fe, I said, assuming that we have *arrived* at a New Western History. We don't have to rehash old ideas and call for new ideas, we can just go ahead and assume that we're finally at our destination, and then we can figure out what we want to do now that we *have* a New Western History. I think, now, that this letter was the private turning point. We no longer had to figure out how to shift gracefully from old ideas to new ideas; we no longer had to try to think fresh thoughts, while also trying to dust off and revitalize old thoughts.

Every professor has probably heard the often-quoted blooper from a student's bluebook: Writing for a course in Renaissance history, some student is supposed to have written, "Dante stood with one foot in the Middle Ages, while with the other he saluted the rising dawn of the Renaissance." Whether or not any student ever wrote the sentence, it is a very apt description of the posture forced on Western historians who were trying to hold the old and the new together, standing with one foot in the Turner thesis, while saluting the rising dawn of ethnohistory and minority history—trying to hold on to the old frontier model, while also trying to make appropriate gestures of recognition and inclusion for Indian, Hispanic, Asian-American, black, Mormon, women's, environmental, and legal history. Or, to apply it even more concretely to Western history, the traditional Western historian stood with one foot on the proposition that the frontier ended in 1890, while with the other he saluted the rising significance of the timber, oil, coal, reclamation, uranium, defense contracting, and automotive Western booms of the twentieth century.

When we dropped the word "toward" from the phrase "toward a New Western history," we allowed Western historians to adopt a far more natural, and comfortable, posture. We could put both feet on the ground of the American West. We could look directly at the continuity between the nineteenth and twentieth centuries. We could pay attention to the convergence of diverse people in the region. We could see the stories that had been lost by the idea of a westward moving frontier line: the northward movement of Hispanics, the eastward movement of Asians, and the prior presence of Indians. We could finally face up to the facts of invasion and conquest, recognizing that Anglo-Americans had to fight both nature and natives before they could impose their versions of property and profit on the West.

If that was the private turning point for a few Western historians, then the public turning point came out of a second stage of correspondence. One of the participants wrote me in response to the letter and asked a perfectly fair question: if we were supposed to assume that we'd arrived at a New Western History, then what might that New Western History be? In reply I wrote a one-page summation of what I thought the new picture was, with the summation hinging on what I've just said—the three C's—continuity, convergence, and conquest.

This has been an exercise in concentration and brevity—first, I write and publish a 350-page book on the reenvisioning of Western history; then, I write and circulate a one-page summation of what the book said; and then, at what I hope is the end of this process of boiling down, I create an alliterative memory-device, reducing 350 pages to three words.

Back at the middle stage, I sent my one-page summation to the "Trails" participants and asked them to do what they wanted with it, agree with it, pick on it, as they wished. And then I took copies of it with me to the "Trails" symposium on the chance that members of the audience would want to know what the phrase "a New Western History" might mean. And then Tom Reid from the Denver Bureau of the *Washington Post* came to the "Trails" conference—to write, I hoped, at least a *word* about the exhibit on which we had worked so hard; but the exhibit went unnoticed, and Reid instead wrote a piece about the new Western History, and in that he quoted from my one-page summation, referring to it as "a paper Limerick distributed at the conference."[1]

I quote that odd line, because it gets at one of the reasons why there are so few public intellectuals. When you try to address a public audience, one of your principal channels of communication is the press. Even though you must rely on the press, you stand a very good chance of coming out looking, not like a wise person distributing the fruits of the university's intellectual labors to a wider audience, but more like a pompous fool. Tom Reid (now, alas, in Japan, with the Denver Bureau of the *Washington Post* shut down, a fact that tells us something) is a fine reporter, and he did the cause of the revitalizing of Western history a world of good with his story. In the meantime, there is that one phrase— "a paper Limerick distributed at the conference"—which, to my ear, carries a chilling image of me, arrayed like a hot-dog vendor or souvenir saleswoman at a baseball game, surrounded by several cardboard boxes full of xeroxes, thrusting copies of a forty- or fifty-page paper on anyone who came within my reach. But all it was, was a one-page hand-out, sitting among many other hand-outs on a registration table, and conference-attenders could pick it up or not pick it up, make it into a paper-airplane or not make it into a paper-airplane, as they preferred; and even though it was modestly subtitled, "Not a Manifesto," it became, almost instantly, against its own will, a manifesto.

I go on about this at some length because it involves the primary peril of the public intellectual, a peril, I suppose, better known to more conventional public officials. In the effort to reach a wider audience, you are very much dependent on the kindness of strangers, and even the kindest of reporters will sometimes make you look like a perfect idiot, or if they cannot get you all the way to perfect idiocy, they will quote you and paraphrase you in ways that make you wince. To all that, after a few moments of self-indulgent wincing, you have to be able to say, "This is bearable price to pay for a worthwhile cause."

A very pleasant stranger from the Associated Press came to interview me last summer, and in our conversation, I referred to the results of a poll the Western historian Carl Abbott conducted in which Western historians were asked on which historians' writings they relied in organizing their courses, and Frederick Jackson Turner and his disciple Ray Allen Billington got a total of eighty-seven votes, with the nearest runner-up, Walter Prescott Webb, trailing more than fifty votes behind. I cited this poll as evidence that there is indeed an *old* Western history; there are a lot of people still loyal to the ideas Turner put forward almost a century ago. And then, even though this pleasant stranger from the Associated Press had a tape recorder present, or at least what *seemed* to be a tape recorder, when her story ran last September, it had this wince-producing sentence in it: "Limerick said a recent poll of regional history teachers showed eighty-seven percent used Turner's theses as the basis for their course."[2]

And so, if one puts any faith in the Associated Press, the conclusion one has to reach is that Limerick cannot tell the difference between "number of votes" and "percentage of votes." Yet if you believe in the necessity of bridging the gap between the university and the public, you have to instantly recover from an injury like this. You have to assume that your friends will know that you are not that dumb, or failing that level of confidence, that they will do you the honor of *asking* you directly if you cannot tell the difference between a vote and a percentage point.

Worse than the Associated Press reporter's creative rendering of my quantitative remarks is one puzzling, and very widespread, response of the press to the changes in Western history—the problem of negativity. After the *Washington Post* ran the story, the *New York Times* was hot on their heels, with a story in December of 1989 that carried the headline "Among Historians, the Old Frontier Is Turning Nastier with Each Revision."[3] Once the *New York Times* had taken up the story, we were launched on a path of publicity as fated as something from a Greek tragedy: *U.S. News and World Report*, the *Los Angeles Times*, the *Christian Science Monitor*, the *Detroit Free Press*, the *Chronicle of Higher Education*, a heavily perfumed fashion magazine called *Elle*, and now even *People*.

What we learned, as one of my colleagues in Western history put it, is that the press mostly covers the press. Everyone did the story, and everyone had to have a hook, and the hook, following on the *New York Times* headline, had to be negativity. "The Old Frontier Is Turning Nastier, Now Historians Are Bad-Mouthing the American Frontier"—that's how the *New York Times* headline-writers supplied the hook.[4]

Those headlines puzzle me. I don't recall ever using the word "nasty," or anything like it; and the first *New York Times* article ends with a quotation from me that seems to contradict the headline:[5]

> I don't think everybody has to buy Kleenex and weep over how unusually unhappy the Western experience was, but it had the usual quota of tragedy and failure, cruelty and inhumanity, and situations of invasion and conquest often raise the stakes on things like that.

So there it is—my wild negativity in a nutshell. In essence, the American West has the same level of moral complexity as the rest of the planet, maybe dramatized a little more because of the process of invaders displacing natives. Who—aside from people with heavy, unexamined emotional investments in a fantasy West—would expect anything different?

This notion of a West turned grim, bitter, sour, ugly was what some reporters wanted to write about; and here the message slipped completely out of my control. Soon any number of reputable people and publications had accepted the press's emphasis on despair and disaster as *my* emphasis. Here, the press was covering the press in an exercise exactly modeled on the children's game of telephone, where you pass on a message, *without* checking back with the original speaker, until the message gets weirder and weirder.

Consider the telephone game played by the magazine *Nieman Reports*, published by a fine program for journalists based at Harvard. The editor at *Nieman Reports* never spoke to me but simply read the article in the *New York Times* Sunday Magazine and then did his or her own creative reading of that piece. In the *Times* report, the *Nieman* editor wrote, "One academic historian sneers at the abandoned mining and ghost towns." The *New York Times* reporter did indeed look at pictures of ghost towns with me, but the reporter never said I sneered at them, because neither he nor anyone else has ever seen me sneer at them. In fact, my point was just the opposite: these relics of failure, of enormous human effort expended in transitory enterprises, deserve to be taken seriously. By some gift of intuition and imagination, the *Nieman Reports* editor knew that I had sneered, and ended his or her summation of the changed picture of Western history with the statement that, contrary to our assertions, the Old West was *not* "all bad-bad-bad."[6]

These are the moments when the practice of American journalism seems "all bad-bad-bad," and the retreat of the public intellectual to the sanctuary of the university seems like a pretty smart idea. If this is what a prestigious press journal like *Nieman Reports* offers in the way of accurate reporting, it does make one a bit fearful about the accuracy of considerably more consequential stories. It begins to seem that the most efficient use of natural resources might be to pick up our morning papers and carry them directly to the recycling box.

But negativity and the *Nieman Reports* aside, most journalists have done a good job by this story. They have brought these ideas to the attention of a much wider audience than we could fit into any university lecture hall. They have shown, moreover, a real thirst for conversation and dialogue with academics. They have, even under the pressure of stern deadlines, done their reading and made it clear that professors who choose to venture out of the university stand a good chance of being welcomed. The door to the university, it turns out, was locked only from the inside, not barred form the outside.

Once I was fully launched on this exercise in media relations, I found that it was my privilege to be misunderstood and misrepresented, not only by journalists, but also by novelists. In the *New Republic* last fall, the novelist Larry McMurtry wrote a curious critique of the New Western History.[7] McMurtry's argument with me was, in some more fundamental way, an argument with his formal self. In a collection called *In a Narrow Grave*, published in the late 1960s, McMurtry had made his own forceful critique of the Western myth's power to mislead. I went back, recently, to read that collection and found there a wonderful essay in which McMurtry describes his experiences as the author of a book made into a movie by Hollywood.[8]

McMurtry's novel *Horseman, Pass By* was becoming the movie *Hud*, with a vast Hollywood crew installed in the Texas Panhandle, with Panhandle matrons circling the filming site and the cast and crew's motel, hoping for a glance of Paul Newman. In one magnificently described scene, McMurtry captured the difficulties of getting Western reality to comply and cooperate with Western mythmaking. Paul Newman was supposed to ride up and discover a dead heifer. Then, in rage at the loss of the cow, he was to look up at a line of buzzards sitting on a tree limb, fire his gun at one of the buzzards, and at that moment, the surviving buzzards were supposed to "soar into the blue Panhandle sky." When McMurtry asked some of the filmmakers "how the buzzard scene had turned out," he was, he wrote, "a little taken aback by the number of stricken looks that turned my way." It seems that the local buzzards—one might say, the natural and indigenous buzzards—that could be lured to the site proved to "be skittery and unphotogenic." And so a dozen buzzards from Laredo, Texas, had to be rounded up and flown "roughly a thousand miles" to Amarillo. But how to get the buzzards to sit on the branch until their cue called for them to soar? "The plan," McMurtry writes, "was to wire the buzzards to a dead tree until they had been photographed; then when Newman shot the gun they could be released electronically."

The plan, as McMurtry puts it, "quite failed to take into account the mentality of buzzards." The buzzards did not take direction well. Wired to the tree they instantly began to try to fly away, and with their feet wired, the effort to fly caused them all to pitch forward. The wires prevented them from flying, but they did not, as McMurtry describes it, "prevent them from falling off the limbs, where they dangled upside down, wings flapping." A dozen buzzards hanging upside down from a tree limb—this is not what Hollywood wants from the West, but this is, nonetheless, what Hollywood had produced.

McMurtry continues the narrative, with the vividness of language that makes one wish he had not chosen, in his recent novels, to devote his talents to the service of the cliches and stereotypes of the "Old, Wild West":

> The buzzards were righted, but they tried again, and with each try their humiliation deepened. Finally they abandoned their effort to fly away and resigned themselves to life on their tree. Their resignation was so complete that when the scene was readied and the time came for them to fly, they refused. They had had enough of ignominy; better to remain on the limb indefinitely.

The filmmakers could release the wire, but the buzzards would not fly. Shouts, firecrackers, a shotgun full of rock salt: they would not move. Eventually some skilled bird-handler was found, and the buzzards at last played their part. But before they gave in and collaborated with Hollywood, the buzzards had offered a useful analogy for the problems of contemporary intellectuals, especially Western historians.

In his *Structure of Scientific Revolutions,* Thomas Kuhn offers the powerful and clear analogy of the earthquake as a model of how intellectual paradigms shift.[9] One paradigm sets the terms of everyone's thinking, but then new evidence, new questions, new issues appear—and stress accumulates like stress along a fault line. When the tension and friction get to a critical point, the earthquake happens, and a new mental landscape, a new paradigm, comes into being.

As far as I can tell, Thomas Kuhn got it right; that is, indeed, how it feels to be involved in a paradigm shift. In the early 1980s, I taught my Western American history course, doing my best to cover the full range of Western American experiences—Indian, Hispanic, French Canadian, Asian, and Anglo. Then, at the end of the semester, I would tell the students to read Frederick Jackson Turner's "The Significance of the Frontier in American History," and, for a final exam question, reinterpret the Turner Frontier Thesis in light of all this new material. The first tremors of the earthquake came, in my case, after I had performed that silly exercise for two or three semesters in a row, and, repeated, that exercise finally made me realize that the old model simply couldn't encompass the new material.

There was no better place to look to see the old paradigm not fitting than the history of Utah. In 1893, when Turner laid out the terms of his Frontier Thesis, he wisely made only one brief, and passing, reference to Utah: "The distinctive frontier of the [midnineteenth century] is found in California, where the gold discoveries had sent a sudden tide of adventurous miners, and in Oregon, and the settlements in Utah."[10] Turner, of course, was arguing that, wherever it was and whoever it involved, the frontier had the same effect: it made Europeans into individualistic, self-reliant Americans. And so Turner wisely kept his reference to Utah *very* brief, a matter of three words, imbedded in a sentence that seems to see the processes of settlement in California, Oregon, and Utah as more alike than different.

That, one could say in hindsight, should have been the end of the Frontier Thesis right then, when the word "Mormonism" failed to make even an appearance. You would think, at the least, that Turner would have brought in Mormonism to reinforce his point that the year 1890 signaled the end of the frontier. Surely the formal end of plural marriage would have given support to the idea of 1890 as a watershed. But including Mormonism for the one or two points in which it *supported* the Frontier Thesis would have left Turner saddled with the many elements of Utah history that *contradicted* his thesis. With or without a three-word reference to the "settlements of Utah," the problem of a paradigm that could not encompass Mormonism did not go away.

On the contrary, when Turner's mid-twentieth-century apologist and defender Ray Allen Billington came up against the problem of Utah, he was even more evasive and dismissive than Turner had been. When Billington wrote a narrative history of the westward movement, he included a chapter on the settlement of Utah. But when he wrote a book to prove that the 1893 Turner Thesis was fundamentally right, Billington left Utah out entirely. Search the index of Billington's *America's Frontier Heritage* for a reference to either Utah or Mormonism, and you find neither. Consciously or not, Billington must have known that Mormons were not going to fit very well in a paradigm that claimed that a uniform, repetitive, standardized frontier process unrolled across the continent.[11]

What would Billington have done with his frontier paradigm if he really had to reckon with Mormon cooperation in irrigated agriculture, with the church's centralized authority in colonization, with federal campaigns against polygamy? Billington and other traditional Western historians were so powerfully in the grip of the frontier paradigm that this question probably never came to their minds. If a Western case study fit their paradigm, it counted, it was significant; and if it contradicted their paradigm, then they might include it unreflectingly in the narrative, but otherwise ignore it completely.

A book like Thomas G. Alexander's *Mormonism in Transition* shows how little bearing the Frontier school had on Utah history. Alexander follows the Latter-day Saints from 1890 to 1930, without any false, distorting sense that Utahans fell over the edge of Western history when they went past the great Turnerian deadline.[12] Western history remains a continuous running story, in a way that it could never be under the Frontier school; and this accumulation of significant events in the twentieth-century West was surely one of the main forces putting pressure on the fault line of the old paradigm.

Kuhn's model of an earthquake is a good one for understanding paradigm-shifts. Still, for the purposes of capturing the *lived* dynamics of the experience, I prefer Larry McMurtry's buzzards—primarily because the earthquake analogy does not leave much room for individual human will, while the buzzard analogy does leave some meaning to individual choice.

This is what it is like to be a part of a scholarly discipline in the late twentieth century: you go to graduate school to have your feet wired to a branch, to learn how people in your field are supposed to see the world. I would not say, on principle, that there is anything wrong with that; it is a perfectly good and desirable thing for people in a field to have some ideas and terms in common. But for Western historians, the process of professionalization meant getting wired up to the term "frontier" and the whole elaborate set of assumptions and premises that word carries. And then, just like the movie-set buzzards, when Western historians tried to fly, the ties holding them to the dead branch of the Frontier school kept them from flying. After several embarrassing tries, they stopped trying and sat, like the resigned, humiliated buzzards, on their increasingly isolated branch, calling out for new models and new approaches but determined *not* to try the unrewarding experiment of flying again.

For all the battiness of the last year's press coverage, this is what has changed in Western history: the wire-binding Western historian to the old Frontier model has been finally, permanently released. It will not be reinstalled; it *cannot* be reinstalled. Anybody who would like to get off the dead tree limb and fly can do that now. But his is not an instant recognition. The first response, I fear, of the birds still on the old tree limb is something closer to envy and resentment. As one bird leaves the tree, the others are inclined to say, "How come *she* can get away with that? How come *she* gets to fly when we're still wired to this old tree?" But they are *not* stuck on the tree anymore. They can fly in any direction they would like.

Here we get back to the perils of public intellectuals. What if they soar off in some direction—and make a mistake? What if they offer some courageous, enterprising big idea about the American West, and it turns out to be less than perfect? There happens to be a clear and easy answer to that question, though I must admit that I did not know that answer when I was writing *The Legacy of Conquest.*[13] I experienced then several bouts of synthesizer's fear: first, the fear that on any page of your synthesis you are discussing something that a dozen specialists know better, and in greater detail, and, second, the fear that those specialists will all descend upon you when the book comes out, pointing out flaws and omissions and errors. In a couple of bouts, the fear nearly paralyzed me; but I now know how unnecessary it was—because there is an easy and effective way of responding on the occasions when your errors are pointed out.

This is what you can do when you have, despite the best of intentions, made an error of omission, or overstatement, or understatement. When someone points this out, you listen, and if what they say seems convincing, you say, calmly, "You know, I think you're right about that; I did overlook the matter you're pointing out, and I'm grateful for your bringing this to my attention." It is remarkable how comfortable this seemingly awkward business can become. To use one or two of the all-too-abundant examples from my own case, *The Legacy of Conquest* mysteriously, inexplicably ignores the Western American fur trade and also Western American cities.[14] When people pointed these two flaws out, I thought, at first, "That can't be true." But I did leave them out, almost entirely. Instead of trying to come up with some unconvincing, defense argument for why I *should* have left them out, a way of pretending that I left them out on purpose, it has been a great relief to say to my critics, "You're absolutely right; the traders and the urbanites should be in there; it would make it a far stronger book."

Is this recognition of how easy it is to admit error any big deal? Does it add up to any real insight? Yes, oddly enough, I think it does. We have, in an unthinking way, adopted a scholarly model of manly combat—when your ideas are criticized, you are supposed to stand your ground and defend your arguments as if they were innocent townspeople and as if you were the sheriff, assigned to protect your vulnerable charges from bullies. The custom of a calm admission of error is by no means the scholar's first response.

The issues of Western American history, and of many other fields of scholarly inquiry, are simply too important, too urgent, to tolerate this kind of intellectual inflexibility. These issues are too important to be muffled by, blunted by, silenced by concerns of ego and thin skin. Comfort, ease, goodwill in admitting error would do an enormous amount to liven up this sport and invigorate both debates among scholars *and* public participation in those debates.

I therefore begin my set of concrete proposals with this suggestion. For every discipline and specialization, let us include in the field's journals a new section. Along with the articles, the abstracts, the book reviews, the list of dissertation topics, let us add the section called "Errors Admitted, Omissions Acknowledged, Oversights Recognized." Whatever our discipline, we all need some formal way to put our admission of error on permanent, accessible record. I, for one, do not want to do a second edition of *The Legacy of Conquest* in which I would make up for these sins of omission against the fur trade, against Western cities, against European ethnicity beyond the distinction of Anglo and Hispanic, and against a number of worthy topics that just did not seem to claim my attention before the final draft went in for typesetting.

Now I get to my eight-part program both for increasing the energy and excitement of scholarly exchange and for increasing the numbers and visibility of Western public intellectuals. What we need, I've concluded, is a restructuring of incentives and rewards. We need professional prizes, prizes you can tell your dean about, prizes you can put on your resumé and count toward your merit raises. Thus my eight-part plan is, in fact, the creation of eight new prizes. I do not want to give too much power to the idea of disciplinary divisions, but it is probably best, if, at first, each discipline or specialization offers its own set of prizes.

These, then, are the prizes.

First, the Prize for the Most Forthright and Graceful Confession of Error. This prize should be easy enough to award, once the journals have their "Errors Admitted" sections in operation. You simply look at the entries in any given year, and there is your pool for choosing the winner.

Second, the Blind Courage of the Synthesizer Award—or, as it will be called in Western history, the Frederick Jackson Turner Memorial Out-on-a-Limb Prize for the young historian who mirrors the young Turner's courage in advancing a big and ambitious model for a whole field. This goes to the individual who, recognizing that nearly every field of inquiry has fractured into many separate, and seemingly unconnected, subfields, tries to put things back together, *not* by cramming the pieces back into the old model, but by fitting the pieces into a new, more interesting, more accurate model.

Third, the Prize for the most Productive, Most Intense, and Most Civil Scholarly Disagreement. This is the one that I hoped to qualify for, but, despite that poll recording eighty-seven votes for Frederick Jackson Turner and Ray Allen Billington as the major thinkers in Western history, I never found anybody in Western history who was interested in a direct debate. So, regretfully, since this is by necessity a two-person prize, I yield to others, with the recognition that it may well be the most important of the prizes, demonstrating the key willingness to make bold statements and to stand up for them. As a current country-western song puts it, "You've got to stand for something, or you'll fall for anything." Productive, intense, *and* civil debate is the best way of putting that proposition into action.

Fourth, the Prize for the Most Dramatic Escape from Specialization. For this prize, and the next one, candidates have to submit before-and-after samples: first, the candidate's work when timidity most tightly tied him or her into a narrow field of inquiry; second, the candidate's work when courage returned, and he or she felt free to draw the most enterprising conclusions from his or her evidence.

Fifth, the Prize for the Most Dramatic Recovery from Academic Jargon. Here, too, we need before-and-after samples, first, of the candidate's prose when imprisoned, and second, of the candidate's prose when liberated.

Sixth, the Prize for the Best Sense of Humor and Greatest Equanimity When Misquoted by the Press While Trying to Reach a Wider Audience.

Seventh, the Most Vigorous Town/Gown Correspondence Prize. For this prize, an academic and a layperson must strike up a correspondence. It doesn't matter who initiates it, but they must exchange at least three thoughtful letters on both sides, or a total of six, with the correspondence from both academic and layperson submitted for judging, and with the criteria for excellence being the ways in which the correspondence builds a bridge between the academic and the interested layperson.

Eighth, the Prize for the Best Demonstration that Communication Is, at the Least, a Two-Way Street. This one goes to the academic who goes out into the world to give a speech and returns to the university having learned something consequential from the people she or he met, with the material thus acquired appearing somewhere—in classroom lectures, in published writing—as proof that this communication went beyond the exchange of pleasantries. Given the shyness of most professors, and given laypeople's fears of academics, winning this prize is not going to be easy.

Once, several years ago, a plumber came to do some repairs. He and I began to talk, and after a few minutes of happy conversation, I made the mistake of referring to "the kids in my class."

"You teach?" he said.

I said, sensing problems ahead, "Yes."

"Grade school?" he said.

"No."

"High school?"

"No, college," I finally had to say, and the plumber instantly said, "Oh, I'm sorry," and I had to work hard and fast to keep him from darting for the door.

What the plumber demonstrated was the common, widespread conviction that conversation with a certified intellectual is a fearful and unnatural act, something that no normal person would undertake unless he or she has been tricked and deceived. It is not going to be an easy matter to qualify for this final prize, since the academic, by definition a shy person, has to undertake to lure other shy people into an activity which they do not, by nature, find comfortable.

It is my hope that candidates from the American West will, at least in the first years, win most of these prizes. It has certainly been my experience, in the last two years, that the conditions in the West are good, close to perfect, for crossing the borders between the university and the rest of the world. I am eager to see these eight prizes instituted, as a way of encouraging a resurgence of the public intellectual. But I must also say that, whether or not these prizes come to exist, the rewards for the activities they are meant to encourage are already enormous. "You must choose between an academic audience and a public audience," a few friends told me when I was writing *Legacy*. As it turned out, I could not choose, and did not choose. I aimed for both audiences, and things turned out wonderfully, wonderfully enough for me to nominate myself as the only author known to humanity who has felt perfectly satisfied with the impact of her book. I have received as much attention as I thought I deserved; I have seen a demoralized field of study change its mood and regain its energy; I have seen a network of bridges built between the public and the universities, bridges that I have been privileged to travel over repeatedly. Enough, then, about the perils of the public intellectual, and on to the privileges.

During the Depression, my grandmothers, one of them in Salt Lake and the other in Brigham City, were both major producers of sandwiches. The troubled people of the Depression, on the road and in need, figured out that these two women were people you could turn to in a pinch—on the corner of 4th South and 5th West in Brigham City, and at 71 M Street in Salt Lake, Ingrid Nelson and Jessie McOwen made sandwiches and gave them to people in need. In fact, my mother remembers, the backyard on M Street had a table and chairs set up for these frequent guests.

This tradition—of responding to people in need, of knowing that the problems of the world are not remote, not dismissible, but immediate, compelling, and requiring a personal response—can also be the privilege of the public intellectual. To stay at home in the university is to turn one's back on urgent problems, to refuse to find out if one could, in fact, be helpful. Keeping the life of the mind shut up in the university, narrowing the currents of academic inquiry into the channels of specialization and jargon, is finally about as senseless an enterprise as if my grandmothers had spent the Depression in their kitchens, making plenty of sandwiches but refusing to go to the door to give them to people in need.

What my Utah grandmothers did in the 1930s was, I realize, much more direct, immediate, useful, concrete—but the privilege of the Western public intellectual is finally this: by taking on the perils of leaving the university, you join the community of Western people who have, over the centuries, helped each other out.

GERALD THOMPSON

The New Western History: A Critical Analysis

In recent years there has developed a historiographical phenomenon that has dramatically affected the writing of frontier-western American history. It goes by the name "New Western History" and claims to have overthrown Eurocentric conceptions about the western movement that have supposedly dominated and corrupted mainstream interpretations since the time of Frederick Jackson Turner—if not earlier. In place of Turner's famous frontier thesis (which declared that the first formative period of American history terminated in 1890), several of the best known of the New Western historians assert a new overarching interpretation about the western expansion of the United States. They feel expansion should be viewed as a harsh conquest of indigenous peoples, Indians and Mexicans, as well as a heavy-handed conquest of the environment—both of which have continued into recent years without interruption by the so-called closing of the frontier. Turner's periodization is discarded as meaningless except as a historical curiosity that blinded Americans to their shortcomings.[1]

At the heart of the New Western History is a view of a regional history that stresses the settlement of the West by Americans as primarily a negative experience for almost everyone involved. David Wrobel, who aptly describes the approach, writes: "Theirs [New Western historians] is a story of tragedy and irony, not triumph. . . . Their story is one of continuous racial oppression and capitalist excess." These historians hope that their analysis will provide a more usable past for understanding and dealing with present-day problems in the West. They claim, among other things, to have supplanted a romantic national myth with a more believable interpretation of the frontier and Western past.[2]

* * *

Before we saddle up for our excursion down the trail of the New Western History, a little background is in order. For quite a few years within the broad field of American history, some students of the West and the frontier felt themselves relegated to secondary roles. During the 1960s and 1970s, many members of the professoriat often regarded the subject matter of the American West as intellectually light with little historical significance or present relevance. This dismissal of frontier/western studies came despite the extraordinary quality of the scholarship being produced by numerous historians. (In fact, the New Western historians would later claim all this path-breaking work as a part of *their* school!) A sense of malaise influenced even the practitioners as they worried about why academic history was ignoring them. The thoughtful would often gather at convention water holes and try to decide what was wrong with western history.[3]

In the 1980s, influenced by currents that had swept other areas of American history, western historians began a formal debate among themselves about the significance of their region, the West, and the nature of the settlement process, the frontier. A similar argument had taken place in the 1930s, but few remembered. ("History doesn't repeat itself, but historians do.") The most outspoken critics were several talented young historians who began to write books and articles that attacked the intellectual paradigms of Frederick Jackson Turner and by implication any historian who had not repudiated Turner's core belief that the frontier had generally been a success for most Americans, shaped our national experience, and disappeared in the late nineteenth century. Their writing was "informed" as they like to say, borrowing the terms of literary analysis, by a new sensitivity to America's shortcomings as demonstrated by the Vietnam War, racism, sexism, and environmental abuse. Although there were only a handful of historians in the 1980s who talked about a New Western History, they were excellent writers, strident in their criticisms, and they made prime copy for the popular media. By the late 1980s, almost every major news publication (*New York Times, U.S. News and World Report, Time,* and *Newsweek*) had carried feature articles on how a new generation of scholars was reinterpreting the frontier/western past. Rising to the bait, the conservative press also joined the fray, usually without realizing the complexity of the arguments encountered.[4]

So just what was it that these scholars had discovered that was supposedly creating such controversy within the ranks of western historians? First, most earlier historians had written about the West from the point of view of national history and thus become apologists for an imperialistic conquest of North America. This viewpoint, dubbed the "triumphalist school" by Patricia Limerick, queen of the New Western historians, had overlooked the great suffering experienced by victims of the white man's "conquest of the West." Previous historians had written about a frontier process and through the use of the word "frontier" the harshness of the *conquest* was lost. Reflecting many currents that could be observed in other parts of academe, the New Western historians charged that earlier historians had neglected Native Americans, Asians, Hispanics, the environment, the labor movement, and women. Standard textbooks such as Ray Allen Billington and Martin Ridge's *Westward Expansion* constituted a narrative that grossly distorted the true nature of the conquest of a continent. Indeed, the work, despite constant revisions to include the latest scholarship, came in for criticism that was second only to that leveled against the original sinner: Turner.[5]

Professor Limerick, the most prominent of the New Western historians, in a widely read book, *The Legacy of Conquest* (1987), as well as in numerous essays, attempted to overthrow the interpretive framework of Turner. In part, Limerick used Turner as a straw man who could be rejected out of hand. Turner had argued that "national character" had been shaped by a frontier experience and concluded that, overall, it was a strength of America. Limerick claimed that failure rather than success should be the principal unifying theme for any history of the West. "This region," she declared, "has had an advanced curriculum in failure"[6]—*failure* rather than "success" because rarely has a nation missed its stated goals as widely as the United States. Historians needed to be present-minded and use their work to address current problems—which many traditional historical practitioners had refused to do for fear of introducing presentist biases.

By concentrating historical studies on the "failures" of the American westering experience, the New Western historians would be able to assert "relevancy" for their work. Curiously, the study of western history was apparently a remote place where ideas took years to reach—for the talk of "relevancy" and "socially useful studies" was reaching frontier/western scholarship about twenty years after it had influenced other realms of American history. Many western historians who would never have labeled themselves as New Westerners were somewhat surprised to learn that intellectual stereotypes (such as white men are evil conquerors and all minorities are saintly victims), increasingly regarded as "clichés" in other areas of history, would gain such recognition. Nevertheless most western historians were delighted that the mass media was talking and writing about how creative the scholarship of the new generation of historians was.[7]

At this point, I'm reminded of Walter Van Tilburg Clark's great novel, *The Ox-Bow Incident.* Two cowboys, Gil and Art, have spent the winter of a Nevada range, and upon entering town for the first time that spring, they find a posse is being gathered to pursue rustlers. Cattle theft, like racism, was such an insidious charge that almost all men, even acquaintances, were suspect until they saddled up to pursue the thieves. Although neither Gil nor Art want to join the posse and both distrust the ringleaders, they decide they'd better go along. Anyone involved with cattle who stayed behind was suspect, and in the climate of the times being suspected of bovine theft could result in fatal consequences. So they join the posse, ride into the mountains, and help lynch several poor characters who later turn out to be innocent and basically good men.

Walter Clark once wrote that the first thing a historian must do is get directly in touch with the past in order to discover the truth about earlier days. But some of the presentist-minded scholars failed to heed Clark's advice to write truthfully about the past and soon began to emulate Clark's fictional characters. A posse of New Western History "wanna be's"—often junior faculty types—joined the ringleaders and hit the trail in search of the villains who thought that "all in all" the American experience produced more good than evil. It was, of course, a politically correct posse (to use modern buzzwords), and for a time I considered calling this article—"P. C. Goes West." Their chief target was, of course, Frederick Jackson Turner. But as you might have guessed a funny thing happened on the way to the hanging tree—the lynching of Turner's ghost proved a far more difficult task than first imagined. If you think such an analogy is exaggerated, here is a quotation from Limerick's *The Legacy of Conquest:*

> The historiographic past does not, after all, provide the firmest ground for launching a defense of professional history. Much of what passed for objective frontier history was in fact nationalistic history, celebrating the winner and downgrading or ignoring the losers. Weighed down by decades of writing in which the bearers of civilization displace unworthy savages, historians cannot overnight achieve a detached, nonpartisan inquiry. Defending the integrity of the profession, one can only hope that one's ethnocentric predecessors can be credibly and rapidly disowned.[8]

* * *

A visit with Professor Limerick now seems like an appropriate stop on our historical truth quest, and we can use the description provided by a journalist from a national publication. Upon entering the prof's domain, the journalist is shown several photos of Colorado's ghost towns, tumbled down and deserted mining camps whose glory days are decades, if not a century, past. Limerick explains the meaning of the towns, which to her are a symbol of the West, particularly the mining West. She infers that in the communities built around the mines, hopes for a wonderful future were laid. Schools were established, and families lived and worked there. But alas the mines failed as they almost always did. Communities were uprooted, and dreams were shattered. This story was often repeated in the West and had supposedly been overlooked by historians. Our western history had been a throw-away history, and just as often "failure" was the ore mined by Americans in the Far West. As you might expect, our reporter has been impressed. He has been thinking about the shortcomings of modern times and now he has heard a historical approach that seems to explain the dismal state of the present, incorporating what he calls a "post-Vietnam mood."[9]

Perhaps as much as anything Limerick has written, this casual description of the meaning of "ghost towns" fascinated me for the insight it provided into the thinking of the best known of the New Western historians. I began to understand why there was such an emphasis on present-mindedness and calls to do away with the concept of objective scholarship. The mining camp story made a good lesson for present problems, but as scholarship it was inaccurate, both in the details and in general conclusions—unless we conclude that *everything* about the past is interpretation.

First, there was the description of mining-camp life. What about those families building for the future with hopes and dreams just like anyone else's? From twenty years of serious study of mining in the Far West, I knew that mining towns were about as unlike eastern communities as one could find. Most mining camps were largely made up of young single men (check the census records), and even major communities such as Tombstone, Leadville, and Bisbee had "sex ratios" that were heavily male. When one looked at the numerous small camps that never achieved a lasting place in western history, one often found a sex ratio in excess of nine males for every female. Even after the turn of century one can locate numerous all-male mining camps in the census records. One doesn't need to have worked under the Berkeley demographers to realize that these communities differed from eastern town and villages.[10]

Then we have the question of mining-camp mentality. Did these young single men, living and working in the most isolated parts of North America, really plan on spending their lives in such an environment? Although some miners may have been "duped" by developers and promoters, most sought the good wages and planned to move elsewhere when mines played out. Many returned to the East. Granted that in the larger mining towns, families and schools could be found, but even then the labor force was overwhelmingly young single males. A present-minded, modern analogy would note those who worked on the Alaskan oil pipeline in the 1970s in a very similar environment. The laborers in the western mining camps in the nineteenth century may have been disappointed when the mines shut down, but they knew enough history to realize that their lives were transient.

After thinking about these mining camps and Limerick's interpretation I found myself agreeing with her that the mining camps were "throw away" communities that in some cases are still damaging the environment down to the present time. No argument there. But she had failed to understand the basic nature of the experience and failed to heed Walter Clark's advice to get directly in touch with the past. Of course, a relativist view of history would state that you've just read two different views about the past that have been shaped by differing views of the present. I feel, however, that we have a factual situation that can be objectively analyzed and tested against the historical record to determine which most closely resembles the nature of the western mining experience.[11]

Relativism has something to do with the New Western History, and perhaps we should not be surprised to learn that the intellectual "wild bunch," as they sometimes call themselves, was heavily indebted to influences of Paul de Man and deconstructist methodology. Limerick especially made use of deconstruction techniques and her work often seems contradictory unless read in light of textual particularism and logocentrism (history is literally the words on the page and nothing else!).[12]

How far away from common sense these historians could stray was illustrated in *The New York Times Book Review* section of March 21, 1993, where Peggy Pascoe noted with satisfaction in a review of Richard Slotkin's *Gunfighter Nation:*

The Myth of the Frontier in Twentieth-Century America that "this book appears at a time when popular enthusiasm for westerns has all but evaporated." Eight days later, Clint Eastwood's *Unforgiven* would gather up four Oscars to add to the box-office success and critical acclaim the film had earlier received. So much for the prof's declaration of the death of the western. Rather than calling themselves the "wild bunch," perhaps the "gang that couldn't shoot straight" would be more appropriate.[13]

* * *

Yet at times I have found myself in agreement with the New Western historians, particularly when they contend that many aspects of western history had been overlooked by Turner and his disciples. However, the revisionists had been at work for decades by the time the phrase New Western History was being used, and an extensive literature on previously ignored aspects of the West had been published. There were good accounts of the role of women, Hispanics, and blacks in the West. Urban history had been discovered, and scholars had begun to illuminate the story of the twentieth-century West—a major shortcoming with Turner's followers. In 1977, an excellent bibliography appeared on the frontier and west as a part of the Goldentree Bibliographies in American History. That study listed 2,973 entries, but the names of Limerick and Co. never surface, and for good reason. The publications of the New Western historians all date from the 1980s forward.[14]

Thus, there was a something of an intellectual cheap shot being leveled at the previous generation of historians. Much of the historical work since the 1950s seemed to fall under the category of New Western History minus the overarching "failure" thesis. And the charges aimed at scholars long deceased rang just a bit hollow since those authors were much closer in time to the nineteenth-century frontier. Moreover, there existed in the criticism a few glaring oversights. For example, California's greatest historian, publisher Hubert Howe Bancroft, never shortchanged or overlooked the Hispanic and Mexican heritage of the Far West. Bancroft's work has had such staying power that sooner or later every serious historian of the West must deal with is publications and his collections. And how could one charge Herbert Bolton with ignoring the Spanish contribution? One might believe that he painted too rosy a picture, but extraordinary scholarship had been produced decades earlier, even in the early part of this century. Native Americans had long received sympathetic treatment from scholars and only in the popular realm did the image of a good civilization confronting the merciless savage have a long run.[15]

Three areas of criticism did seem valid—women had received little attention in western history until the 1960s, important aspects of the twentieth-century experience had been neglected, and environmental history was a recent phenomenon. Yet, the whole historiographical development of writing about the frontier and the West seemed to me to have been more evolutionary than revolutionary—it reflected the gradual extension of historical studies into new, unexplored areas that help us to understand the full nature of the regional experience, the national experience, the ethnic experience, the female experience, and any other experience. In fact, there had been an explosion of scholarship, and in *The Chronicle of Higher Education,* Limerick would write that if you disagreed with her it was because you had become cranky from trying to keep up with your field. Actually, there was little disagreement with the most of the scholarship—I made a modest contribution to revisionist history myself. The intellectual disagreement is with the negative thesis that the New Western historians would impose by edict rather rigorous scholarship.[16]

But as the volume piled up, something else could be observed—the authors regularly did not give their primary allegiance to either regional or frontier history. Their primary identification came from a specialty, such as women's history, environmental studies, Native American studies, etc. The umbrella of the frontier that had been a unifying theme no longer seemed applicable. Hadn't many people long ago discarded most of Turner's specific notions about the frontier?

Indeed, as more native westerners began to write history,

the region itself seemed like a better vehicle for thematic unity, but regional definitions proved elusive. Strangely, as several of the New Western historians claimed to be writing regional history, their emphasis still focused on the process of change and deciding whether the change was "good." Because the biggest force for change was the entrance of Americans into the region, the scholarship often still concentrated on the story of Anglo-Americans victimizing everyone in the West, including themselves and the environment. One of my colleagues at the University of Toledo sees this neo-puritan influence on American scholarship as the loudest of the new breed of scholars tries hard to write jeremiads about history in order to save the present.

To my way of thinking there was an element in the New Western history that was almost racist and sexist. For example, individuals like Bancroft and Charles Lummis, just to mention two names, believed that an Anglo-Californian acquired a heritage that was not simply carried in the individual's genetic formula by DNA molecules. Regionalism was more inclusive. Californians or New Mexicans must embrace a heritage that was an amalgamation of Indian, Spanish, and Mexican, in addition to the dominant heritage from the eastern states. I embraced this view and felt a strong allegiance to regional studies over the "frontier" process, and consequently found myself grouped in a marginal way with the New Western historians. Because of the previously mentioned media attention, I was happy when colleagues noticed that my work had become "cutting edge," but at least one perceptive book reviewer noted that my contribution to Limerick's volume *Trails: Toward a New Western History* was significantly different from the others.[17] As I don't want to hamper a young man's career by praising his work, I'll just note that he read my essay and observed that it stood alone in *Trails* in viewing the western American story as more of a success than a failure. This was a correct reading; for after rejecting many parts of Turner's thesis, I ultimately arrived at agreement with Turner's general proposition that westering proved beneficial for most Americans. Perhaps it was not quite a triumphal journey from East to West, but in our national life and in the lives of most individuals who went West the story was more optimistic than Limerick and Co. had explained.

Much of the new scholarship bolstered my position. One could look for example at R. A. Burchell's excellent social history of the San Francisco Irish community and learn that in the case of that city, the Turnerian view of opportunity and the frontier coincided. Asian studies revealed that the Chinese who came to Gold Mountain as they called California didn't find much gold, but they did prosper even when discrimination and legal restrictions placed them at the bottom of society. Women, of course, would be granted the vote in the Far West—fifty years before the passage of the nineteenth amendment—and they would assume occupational careers denied them in the East. Latinos, principally Mexicans, in the early twentieth century would flee Mexico and take jobs that were usually low paying, but so much better than those in their homeland that occasional talk of building a wall along the southern border of the United States would surface. Even American Indians who had suffered more than any other group from the conquest of the West found themselves in the late twentieth century digging their way out from the cultural avalanche that had threatened to bury them. Tribal life continued and strengthened, and recent decades found that the American legal tradition, which had been imposed by conquest, could also serve the interests of Native Americans. Lawsuits were filed against state and federal governments by tribes, and Indians began to win redress in court.

Consequently, I was at a loss to see the American experience in the West as more evil than not; it did not take a Ph.D. in history to recognize that the West had enriched the nation to such an extent that our international position as a world power was predicated upon nineteenth-century expansion. I've often wondered if the New Western historians would have preferred a profoundly weaker United States in the global rivalries of this century. When one visits the Indian reservations and sees the well-tended cemeteries with their abundance of small American flags over the graves of veterans one senses that these people, the first human residents of the region, have grasped a historical truth far better than many academics; but I recognize that patriotism, particularly as demonstrated by military service, is not a sentiment shared these days by many academic historians. Of course, when one travels through the dynamic cities of the West—San Diego, Seattle, Phoenix, or Denver—one must really dismiss a great amount of evidence in order to find failure—problems in abundance most certainly—but out and out failure, hardly. Thus, antiquated Frederick Jackson Turner had come closer to the truth, despite all his flaws, for he had told a story about progress and success; and in fairness to Turner he always showed himself to be open to new forms of scholarship and to revision and modification of his own work.

I admit, however, that I like the New Western historians' emphasis on continuity and their recognition that the so-called closing of the frontier in 1890 did not constitute a climactic watershed in American history. I don't know if such a view is sufficient to gain for me the mantle of a New Western historian for I also know that Turner repeatedly try to de-emphasize the importance of the frontier and boost his essay, "The Significance of Section in American History." But the word "frontier" was magical for many Americans; it conjured up images of brave individuals battling against a savage environment in order to bring the light of civilization into the wilderness. The image was as old as the first European settlements in the New World and became firmly imbedded in American mythology during the nineteenth century. One should never forget that the western movement of the 1800s took place within an intellectual climate of romanticism, which may well prove impossible to discard. Turner's famous essay on the frontier, which is the most lasting piece of historical scholarship ever written by an American, put the myth into an academic paradigm.[18]

It is not surprising that Turner provided an easy target for criticism. He wrote almost nothing about the Far West, and his frontier, with evolutionary stages of development, works much better for the Midwest than for my region, the Far West. It seems inappropriate when applied to the mining West or the pastoral West. Nor does it account for the dominant role played by the federal government in the lives of Americans in the region from the 1800s forward. And, of course, there is little in Turner about Indian and Hispanic heritage, liberated women, or the urban oasis culture. In so many specifics, Turner seems to have been wrong, except in the greatest of his generalizations. What was happening worked well for most Americans, and as a result Turner's story of success is still more believable than the catalog of failures coming from the New Western History.

So far, I have only mentioned the name of the most prominent of the New Western historians, Patricia Limerick. She deserves the attention because her writings have received wide circulation. Yet, upon close examination Limerick has much in common with Turner. In fact, Limerick touts herself as a regionalist but fails to give full treatment to those whose story has not yet been told. Her anecdotal stories in *Legacy of Conquest* are generally those of white males and in no case are minorities or victimized characters brought to center-stage and allowed to make decisions that affect their own history. Minorities are victims and even some white males are victims. Curiously, this goes against much of the best scholarship of recent years, which sees Native Americans, Asians, Hispanics, and women as having a significant impact on their own historical experience. Second, Limerick uses the word "conquest" in place of Turner's frontier and sees a conquest that has continued down to recent times without a break when the frontier supposedly "closed." But by focusing on an on-going "conquest" that continues over several centuries is one not, therefore, focusing on *process* rather than place. If you write a book that emphasizes the continuity of change, have you not elevated the *process* above the *region*, regardless of what you choose to term the process. This illustrates the difficult task faced by regionalists who hope to develop a broad interpretation for the West—how to emphasize regionalism over the frontier.

If I could cast a vote for my favorite New Western historian, it would surely be for Richard White. Like many of this group, White seems to have been intellectually formed by the turmoil of the 1960s, but unlike some of the New Westerners, White's serious intellect generally rises above presentism to see the complexity of historical issues. Recently, White authored a text entitled: *"Its Your Misfortune and None of My Own:" A New History of the American West.* There is much to praise in the book. It is extensively researched and may well become a standard textbook. But as a regional history, there is a real problem. White's book is about the American West and begins with Lewis and Clark—with only passing mention of Spain, Mexico, and Indians (the latter omission is curious because White is an extraordinary scholar of Native America). Again, one finds a similarity with an older Turnerian approach. Even the often maligned text *Westward Expansion* makes a better effort to provide serious treatment of Spain and Mexico in the Far West. What White does is excellent, but it doesn't quite fill the bill as a regional history—process still reigns supreme, and in this case the process doesn't pay sufficient attention to the regional antecedents to the United States. Moreover, the economic and business history of the region is seen within a neo-Marxist frame of greed and exploitation, hardly an accurate or balanced view.[19]

The third and last historian of the Big Three of New Western History is Professor Donald Worster of the University of Kansas. Worster's writings illustrate the best and worst traits of the genre. No living or dead historian has argued as thoughtfully, passionately, or eloquently as Donald Worster in stating the case for the West as a distinct region. Several years ago, he wrote an article entitled "New West, True West," which was so well conceived and executed that it stands as something of a mission statement for a regional approach to the West. But like Limerick, Worster subscribes to the concept of "relevancy and the usable past," and he has defined history in such a way as to preclude the work of most historians, including myself, from his definition of history. Worster has stated that history is a tool to solve current problems, and a historian should confront problems, analyze how they have developed, and even offer tentative solutions. He also describes himself an "essentialist," believing that the most important things we can study are those that are essential to our lives as individuals, but especially as a species called *homo sapiens*. For Donald Worster, the essentialist, nothing is more basic than the environment and as a consequence he is regarded as a leading environmental historian. When the essentialist approach is combined with Worster's study of the West as a region, there can be only one subject worthy of study—water. (At a recent conference Worster was asked about the importance of biography in history, and he stated that he did not consider biography to be history—individual lives were insignificant in the face of movements and forces.)[20]

Worster bases his approach to the history of water in the West on a priori assumptions. First, people must live in harmony with nature. Second, a large population in an arid environment is unnatural because a renewable, nondepleting supply of water cannot be found in close proximity. Third, governments control people in arid regions by monopolizing water resources and dictating consumption and usage. Fourth, a day of reckoning will someday come (echo of jeremiad scholarship!). All of these points to me have more of a New Age popular culture wisdom about them rather than academic insight, but Worster assures us that he first gleaned these nuggets in a book entitled *Oriental Despotism* written in 1958 by Karl Wittfogel. After reading Wittfogel, our Kansas professor realized that the U.S. federal government through vast reclamation projects had created a water empire in the West that rivaled anything the Manchu dynasty ever presided over. Worster's most famous work, *Rivers of Empire*, charts the history of Uncle Sam's aqueous kingdom.[21]

As is so often the case with the New Western History, I find much that I like in Worster's work. As a native westerner I especially admire the ploy of citing a bulky, somewhat obscure work and claiming it as a fount of inspiration for ideas that are uttered by tens of thousands of common citizens without Ph.D. after their names. Worster's general observation that something is wrong with federal water policy that subsidizes agribusiness with cheap water will not be defended by this historian. But I find the idea that living in an arid region is unnatural to be simply an author's belief or prejudice. Frankly, after spending much of my early life in Tucson, Arizona, I find living in the Midwest in winter for the last fifteen years to be highly unnatural. I suppose the only natural place for human habitation would be those few areas of the globe with ideal climates where one would need no artificial habitation, with sufficient food, requiring little exertion to obtain. We certainly wouldn't want to have to engage in something as unnatural as work. I could continue, but as you can see I have fundamental essentialist differences with Worster's premises.

But let's look for a minute or two at the actual history of the federal government and water in the West. I went to Worster's book with two questions in mind. First, why did the federal government adopt the water policy that dominated the twentieth century? Second, how successful was the federal government in meeting its goals? I must admit that I was not too surprised to discover that Worster gives almost no space in his book to these two questions. Although no scholar has as yet studied these subjects in depth, I can give you some preliminary answers. First, it was feared that an agricultural shortage could develop in the United States and that new agricultural lands would be necessary in the future if the American population and economy were to continue to expand. None other than Frederick Jackson Turner, who was always reading the latest government statistical report, saw a drop in agricultural production as a harbinger of starvation in the cities—if the trend continued.[22] And even if a crisis was not so imminent, inexpensive food and clothing (cotton is very water intensive) offered immense economic advantages to the United States on the world market as well as the obvious advantages to individual Americans. It should also be pointed out that in order to establish the water empire in the West, the cooperation of the eastern public was essential. Unlike the Oriental despotism model, an imperial decree from Emperor Roosevelt 1 would not find Congress kowtowing.[23]

Finally, there was another very practical reason for reclamation projects—flood control. Every few decades, western rivers, particularly, the Colorado River, would rampage out of control and destroy communities along the banks. There would be an extensive loss of lives, and property worth millions of dollars would be destroyed. In severe cases the flooding could be sufficiently damaging to affect the national economy. Strangely, Worster makes no mention in his book of the need for flood control—I suppose "flooding" is natural.

Well, these were the two questions that I brought to Worster's book and neither were really addressed. I had to look elsewhere to find out that major flooding on the Colorado, for example, has been greatly diminished, and by almost any standard western reclamation has become a cornerstone of American agribusiness —the only part of the American economy that always shows a favorable balance of trade, and of course the cost of living in the United States is the lowest of any major industrial nation. All these benefits, however, do no negate Worster's principal point that at present there is a problem with water policy; but a fuller discussion of the issue's history and complexity, I feel, would ultimately serve better toward developing a more rational policy.

Donald Worster is definitely at his best when delineating conspiracies between evil corporations and the government. Like the other New Western historians he does not allow for the possibility of any beneficial effect from the movement of capitalism into the West, even though most Americans, including the supposedly conquered minorities, have benefited form the business activity. When Worster turns philosophical, however, one finds his comments riveting, as when he urges historians to "examine humane behavior from a nonhuman perspective—to look, as it were, through the eyes of the rest of nature."[24] He is the only historian that I know holding a major professional appointment who believes that he can speak the language of trees and rocks. I suppose a conservative view may well come forth and argue that most trees felt a sense of noblesse oblige toward humans and offered themselves as willing sacrifices for home and fuel. Limerick also adds her words of wisdom on the subject of the environment: "Euro-American colonization was at its core an 'assault' on trees." So much for uplifting the role of minorities and women in the story of the West—they have now been reduced in significance to rank somewhere below the importance of lumber and firewood.[25]

Initially, I had hoped to concentrate most of this chapter on the fringes of the New Western History, because it is out on the edge where you'll find the preposterous and humorous. However, it seemed more important to devote the bulk of my attention to the key scholars who will probably exert a wide influence for many years. Nevertheless I want to mention briefly a new hobby I've developed that relates to this subject. In the past few years, I've taken to going to sessions in other academic disciplines that relate to the American West, and I'd like to detail a few of these findings. In April 1992, for example, I attended several of the American Indian Studies sessions at the Western Social Science meeting in Denver. In one discussion the panelists asserted that prior to the arrival of Europeans the Native Americans possessed no weapons of war and "lived in a Paradise." Timothy Baylor of Amarillo College, not realizing that he was hearing a party line, attempted to disagree and was attacked for holding an ethnocentric basis. In a different session, George Tinker presented a paper on Indian religion and explained that it is im-possible to communicate any degree of understanding within the framework of a conference or a classroom. He noted that these are institutions of western civilization and the western format shapes the content. He went on to express doubts about the value of American Indian Studies programs because knowledge possessed by Indians cannot be communicated through words. Administrators looking for a willing target for the budget axe might well consider Mr. Tinker's observations and proceed accordingly.[26]

From American studies, particularly in the deconstructionist image of the West, I learned that all male scholars of the West are homosexuals with a death wish. This impressive insight comes from Jane Tompkins in her articles and especially her book *West of Everything* (1992). She calls us worshippers of the phallocentric myth and states that, by gender, men are unable to write about the region in any other fashion. She observes, "The western is secular, positivist, and antifeminist; it focuses on conflict in public space, is obsessed by death, and worships the phallus." She repeats the juvenile assertion that western literature's fascination with guns is phallic in origin and even the western landscape with an emphasis on towering buttes and open spaces is phallocentric. This interpretation counters the older interpretation that the region is feminine and virgin—an earlier idea about the western myth and novel. Whether or not Tompkins is correct (she is married, by the way, to Stanley Fish, high priest of political correctness at Duke University), I found her work most amusing.[27]

For those of you interested in this new approach to western literature, it might be well to consider again the role of the East. In reading Jane Tompkins, I realized that there exists an eastern novel that is exactly the opposite of the western. Rather than taking place in the open, the eastern novel is primarily set indoors—in rooms that often become overheated and are crowded with people, almost all women, who engage in endless discourse until the principal character arrives at the point of exhaustion. Sometimes, she even faints. It is clear to me now that these eastern novels, particularly of the late nineteenth and early twentieth century, are directly analogous to westerns. Thus, I give you a new paradigm for understanding these novels, the vaginal-centric, lesbian East. Why is it that our serious scholarship in history is not this much fun? If we can just borrow the tools of the literary deconstructionists, think what we might accomplish as historians.[28]

Related tangentially to the deconstructionist approach are some peculiar twists within the logic of some of the New Western historians. When their work is criticized for factual mistakes, they fall back upon the relativity of truth, but they will not extend the same courtesy to earlier writers. Doesn't the abandonment of "any measure of historical objectivity" allow that the frontier hypothesis is still valid if one wants to believe it? Limerick stated in a radio broadcast that the battle against Turner had been won, but how could such a thing be in a relativists world view?[29] Gerald Nash, who I believe is one of this nation's greatest historians, comments: "To teach America's youth exclusively about the alleged depravity of the Western experience is to do a disservice to the profession. If the theory of generational change has any validity, the negative views of the past thirty years will soon run their course."[30]

* * *

So in conclusion, is there a New Western History? Yes, but it has evolved slowly over the decades in a process that is evolutionary and would encompass hundreds of historians who have written about the western experience. To state what should be obvious, modern historians see frontier/western history differently than did those of a hundred years ago, and new themes and subjects that were previously ignored have received attention in hundreds, if not thousands, of books and articles. Has the New Western History developed an interpretative framework that supplants the old frontier model? The best answer seems to be not yet, and maybe never. There still exist widespread difficulties in defining the West as a cohesive historical entity, although progress is being made in that direction. Finally, although Turner's frontier thesis has suffered critical and insightful attacks, he still offers a process that is unfolding even in present days. Turner's emphasis upon success still comes closer to reflecting regional history, even in the late twentieth century, than does the characterizations of "failure" that several of the self-proclaimed New Western historians attribute to our region's past.

If a new general interpretation is to emerge about the nature of the westering experience, it must encompass the history of all of the actors in the story. *Success* as well as *failure* must be indicated. Minorities should be given their proper role as people who have played an important part in shaping the region's history and were not simply victims. What might be the look of a new synthesis for western history? In its narrative form, Kevin Starr's multivolume intellectual history *Americans and the California Dream* offers a possibility. His work is complex and never forgets that the dream of a better life for all has not been fulfilled. He writes of California's history:

> Of course, the dream outran the reality, as it always does. California experienced more than its share of social problems because its development was so greedy and unregulated. No evocation of imaginative aspiration can atone for the burdens of the California past, especially the violence and the brutality. Acknowledging the tragedy, however, Californians must also attune themselves to the hope. The struggle for corrective action in the face of history put earlier generations in touch with their best selves. What they attained, attained in the struggle and the dreaming, deserves our respect—and our most sincere celebration.[31]

Julius Lester, African-American historian and novelist, observes, "I think where it [New History] has erred is that the line between correction and condemnation became very thin. . . . I think we should be mature enough as a nation to put all the stories together and say, 'Yeah, this is great about America, and this hurts.' It's not either/or."[32]

CARL ABBOTT

The American West and the Three Urban Revolutions

The American West of the 1990s is the product of three eras of city building. From the eighteenth century to the present, three distinct urban systems and types of city have reflected the successive urban revolutions that have structured and restructured the forms and patterns of world settlement. The first era of substantial urbanization and economic change stretched from the Spanish reconquest of New Mexico in the 1690s to the founding of Sitka in 1804 and contemporaneous Anglo-American efforts to place permanent settlements along the Columbia River. The second era of intensive urbanization and regional growth stretched form the 1840s to the 1890s. The third era has been playing itself out since World War II in communities and hinterlands from Austin to Anchorage.

Cities have been the gateways between the western frontier and the world, mediating the region's evolving relationships with the dominant actors in the global economy. They have been the entrepôts that have centralized the exchange of regional resources for finished goods. New westerners have entered the region through its cities—along the royal highway from central Mexico to Santa Fe, on the Katy Railroad from St. Louis to Dallas, through the international air terminal at LAX. The specific steps through which Denver emerged as the capital of a Rocky Mountain Empire or Spokane assisted the growth of the Inland Empire of the Columbia Plateau are parts of the continuing process by which the far corners of the American West have been linked to the evolution of European capitalism into global capitalism. Cities and systems of cities have made the "rise of the West" as an episode of American history part of the global process that William McNeill summarized in *The Rise of the West.*[1]

No single framework, of course, can encompass it all. Every synthesis highlights certain aspects of the historical experience and shrugs off others. Nevertheless, an urban system model offers a number of advantages for organizing the history of the nineteen westernmost states of the United States. In several ways, it falls clearly on the side of the "new" western history of the 1980s and 1990s by showing that the textbook frontier of the mid-nineteenth century was a specific product of processes far larger in both space and time. As in other new interpretations of the West, key words are continuity and connections.[2]

- The model highlights the direct connections between the development of the West and larger historical changes such as mercantile imperialism, industrialization, and the rise of an informational economy. It helps us to situate the West at the crossroads of the modern world. We can see Texans, Montanans, and Alaskans not only as American westerners but also as western *North* Americans who share common histories with Mexico and Canada, as Pacific Americans who share a common history with Australasia and the Pacific islands, and as peripheral Americans who share a common history with American southerners. The West as structured by its urban systems now spans the Atlantic and the Pacific economies, stands balanced on the border between the rich global North and the poorer South.
- The model links the eighteenth and twentieth centuries in a single analytical structure and suggests appropriately heavy emphasis on the twentieth. Without ignoring the nineteenth century, it places the decades of initial English-speaking settlement within a larger framework rather than picking out the conquest of the western frontier as a free-standing historical subject.
- The model's central concern with economic growth and the changing distribution of population emphasizes the essentials of traditional frontier history. However, it also draws attention to cities as arenas for exploring conflict and accommodation among classes, races, and ethnic groups. For the twentieth century, it helps to explain many issues of environmental change as the result of urban demands for previously rural resources.

- The study of cities has been more prominent among social scientists and cultural critics than western historians. A focus on urban systems can enrich historical analysis by introducing the theories and findings of other disciplines, especially as they relate to modernization and economic hegemony.

Urban Revolutions and the Global System

Three types of city have appeared in sequence over the past five millennia—preindustrial cities, industrial cities, and a currently emerging form that we can tentatively call postindustrial. Each type is associated with a global shift in the balance between urban and nonurban population. Its emergence has involved revolutionary changes in settlement patterns and social institutions.

The era of preindustrial cities embraces most of the history of literate civilization. Between 3500 and 500 B.C., inhabitants of the Middle East, India, China, and middle America independently created cities as the social machinery to organize the benefits of economic specialization. Preindustrial cities were distinguishable from agricultural villages by the preponderance of nonagri-cultural specialists such as craftsmen, merchants, and officials; by their literate elites; and by the development of systems of administration or government for gathering surplus production from a substantial hinterland.

Preindustrial cities were large only in comparison to rural villages and crossroads hamlets, with populations measured in the thousands or tens of thousands. Only exceptional cases, such as Imperial Rome, Abassid Baghdad, and Chang'An under the T'ang Dynasty, reached half a million. In contrast, Medicean Florence was smaller than present-day Boise. The builders of the Cologne Cathedral lived in a town smaller than Great Falls. As late as 1800, Europe contained only four cities with populations greater than 100,000.[3] Cities in preindustrial societies accounted for only 2 to 10 percent of total population but housed nearly all of the historical actors—kings, philosophers, merchants, prelates. Most city dwellers served the needs of the religious and political elites. In turn, the elites supported their cities by gathering the surplus of surrounding territories through trade, tribute, and taxation, structuring societies or empires into economies of unequal exchange.[4]

Over the past five millennia, we can trace the gradual extension of this territorial reach with new technologies of warfare and communication. Bronze-age cities such as Babylon and Knossos reached tens or hundreds of miles into their hinterlands. An iron-age capital like Rome could reach more than a thousand miles in every direction, exercising its influence through a hierarchy of smaller towns. As late as the thirteenth century, the heartland of Eurasia fell into eight regional circuits of urban influence and trade—London to Venice, Alexandria to Aden, Damascus to Hormuz, and so on to the east. By the sixteenth and seventeenth centuries, in contrast, sail-age cities like Lisbon and Amsterdam were able to extend the influence of mercantile capitalism into thinly articulated but far-flung patterns of global influence that Immanuel Wallerstein has characterized as the first world-system. The anchors at the far ends were European military and trading towns from Bahia and New Amsterdam to Malacca and Batavia.[5]

If the era of preindustrial cities is measured in millennia, industrial cities are the distinctive product of the nineteenth century. The industrial city was "invented" in Manchester and London, imitated in France and Germany, and exported to the United States. The British census of 1801 found only one city over 100,000, housing 5 percent of the kingdom's population. There were 35 such cities by 1901 with 26 percent of the population. Industrializing nations shifted from largely rural to substantially urban societies in the course of two generations. The rate of urbanization reached its peak in Britain between 1800 and 1850, in Germany and the United States between 1850 and 1890, and in Japan between 1870 and 1920.[6]

As early as 1832 the *Manchester Guardian* was asserting that "the manufacturing system as its exists in Great Britain, and the inconceivably immense towns under it, are without parallel in the history of the world." The new industrial city threatened social disintegration, political revolution, and moral degradation. It was also the "very symbol of progress, foremost in the march of improvement, a grand incarnation of progress."[7] The climax products of this second urban revolution were the teeming manufacturing and commercial cities that crowded northern Europe, Japan, and parts of eastern North America at the opening of the twentieth century—Glasgow, Essen, Osaka, and Pittsburgh as well as London, Berlin, Paris, and New York.

The explosive growth of industrial cities required the incorporation of new territories and populations into the industrial system as suppliers of resources and markets for manufactured goods. The result was a new global geography that Wallerstein termed the second world-system. The Atlantic core nations controlled the periphery through a greatly expanded network of colonial cities in Africa and Asia and quasi-colonial cities in the Americas. In the world economy, Bombay, Melbourne, Denver, San Francisco, and the fictional Sulaco of Joseph Conrad's *Nostromo* played essentially the same role. They facilitated the entrance of European capital, organized access to regional markets, and funneled regional products to factory cities on both sides of the North Atlantic.[8]

The last half century has brought a third restructuring of urban form and functions on the world scale, with Calcutta, Mexico City, and Los Angeles replacing Manchester and Chicago as the symbols of the urban era. New technologies and institutions of communication have bought people more and more easily into a single marketplace for ideas as well as goods, driving a further integration and elaboration of the global system of cities. Most obvious has been the explosive urbanization of the southern two-thirds of the globe. UN projections suggest that the aggregate urban population of the developed nations will double from 389 million to 784 million between 1960 and 2000. The urban population of less developed nations is expected to more than quadruple over the same period, from 371 million to 1,553 million. By 1980, developing countries accounted for fifteen of the twenty-five largest metropolitan agglomerations.[9]

In the developed world, the ongoing revolution in urban technology is bringing a new balance of centralization and decentralization. Settlement patterns have loosened to the extent that the commuting zones of individual cities are now measured in hundreds of miles.[10] At the same time, corporate and financial control has concentrated in a handful of "world cities." At the steps below the global capitals, changes in trade, financial systems, and travel have vastly extended multilateral ties within and across national systems of cities. Brussels and Bahrain, Miami and Montreal, Honolulu and Houston are all specialized players in the urbanized world.[11]

If All the West Were San Antonio

The history of San Antonio encapsulates the impact of the three urban revolutions on the American West. Twenty-five years ago, Sam B. Warner, Jr., published a key article entitled "If All the World Were Philadelphia: A Scaffolding for Urban History." The article offered a periodization for the history of American industrial cities and pointed to an essential set of variables for comparative study.[12] The history of San Antonio (or San Francisco or St. Louis) over three periods of urbanization provides the same sort of scaffolding for understanding the development of the American West. San Antonio originated as a political outpost of a European trading empire in the eighteenth century. American industrialization after 1850 transformed it into a regional center that fed western resources into the national economy. In turn, the economic transformations of the later twentieth century have made it a direct participant in the defense, information, and international economies that have marked the maturation of the old American frontier into the new American Sunbelt.

San Antonio owes its existence to a self-conscious effort to project Spanish imperial power. The town's first civil settlers in 1731 were Spanish subjects from the Canary Islands, transplanted 5,000 miles as an act of global empire-building. Their job was to support an existing mission and presidio. Perched astride the road from Mexico to the political frontier in East Texas, San Antonio became the center of the thinly scattered settlements of Spanish Texas. It thrived between 1762 and 1802 as the center for a ranching industry that served markets in Louisiana.[13]

San Antonio typified the European penetration of western North American during the "long eighteenth century," a period I've named on the analogy of the "long sixteenth century" described by historians of early modern Europe. In the European case, the term encompasses thirteen decades of economic expansion from the Columbian voyages to the Thirty Years War that saw the formation of Wallerstein's first world-system. In the American instance, the term captures the century and a quarter during which that same world-system tentatively incorporated the western third of the North American continent. Spanish, French, Russian, and English officials and merchants began to add the future American West into the multinational commercial system centered on the North Atlantic.[14] In particular, the frontier towns tied native populations into the trading circuit of mercantile capitalism as suppliers of furs and hides.

The era began with the Spanish reconquest of Santa Fe and the upper Rio Grande between 1692 and 1694. It spanned the European settlement of Texas, southern Arizona, and California and the definition of the *Provincias Internas* as a distinct border region in 1776. It also encompassed the planting along the Mississippi River of French settlements whose trading interests looked westward across the prairies. It ended in the early nineteenth century with the establishment of Russians at Sitka and the start of continuous British and American trading settlements in the Columbia River basin. San Antonio, Nacogdoches, Albuquerque, Tucson, Los Angeles, Monterey, and St. Louis all trace their origins to this long eighteenth century of mercantile imperialism.

The early Spanish and French communities fit easily into the model of preindustrial cities described by sociologist Gideon Sjoberg. Both nations laid out central plazas surrounded by churches and other public buildings. The famous Laws of the Indies prescribed the ideal form for Spanish towns, as followed in communities like San Antonio. From Montreal to New Orleans to St. Louis, French settlers built essentially the same sort of community centered on a riverfront plaza. Dependence on animal power and travel by foot meant compact settlements with houses built to the street lines. In contrast to large agricultural villages like Acoma or Zuni, new communities such as Santa Fe matched the standard definition of "city" that social scientists have derived from the study of early China and the Middle East. They housed a religious and political governing class that controlled nearby agricultural communities. Protected by professional soldiers and served by specialized craftsmen, the elites utilized the surplus of the immediate hinterlands in return for protection and cultural services.[15]

High tide for this first urban system in western North America was the start of the nineteenth century. European conflicts pushed the French out of the last of their American colonies after 1800, Spanish expansion stopped, and Americans, British, and Russians all found it difficult to build on their footholds on the North Pacific coast. After the Louisiana Purchase, the United States confined itself to official and unofficial exploration . Lewis, Clark, Pike, Long, Schoolcraft, and Frémont reported on resources and routes of access. So did the merchants in fur and hides who began to operate out of the Louisiana territory. Neither the American explorations nor the redrawing of political geography, however, had substantial effects on the eighteenth-century system of towns and trade through the 1810s, and 1820s, and 1830s.

The second era of western urbanization coincided with what Eric Hobsbawm calls the Age of Capital—the years from 1848 to 1873 when a sustained economic boom drew much of the work into a highly integrated economic system.[16] Mass production and marketing of manufactured goods required massive flows of raw materials from India, Southeast Asia, and the Americas. In the United States, the Age of Industry brought the coalescence of an industrial core anchored by New York and Chicago. Between 1850 and 1890, the second urban revolution transformed the northeastern ports into industrial centers and built a network of new factory cities along the Great Lakes and Ohio Valley. It simultaneously placed new demands on internal trade and on the primary products of the western territories.[17]

In the American West, this era of growth began with the expansion of U.S. territory through conquest and negotiation between 1845 and 1867. Economic change came in a rush. Newcomers transformed the towns of Mexican California into American cities.[18] They planted thousands of new settlements that yielded up hundreds of new cities and a score of new metropolises. Within the space of a generation—from the heyday of the Oregon Trail in 1843 and 1844 to the transcontinental railroad of 1867—American settlers built the outlines of a new urban system.

Historian Rodman Paul and geographer Donald Meinig have provided complementary frameworks for understanding the urban system of the mid-century West.[19] Paul focused on the organization of the mining regions by two sets of cities. San Francisco dominated the economy of the Pacific slope through a handful of secondary cities like Sacramento, Stockton, and Portland and scores of smaller mining towns. A second system connected Chicago and St. Louis to Denver and the mining towns of the Rocky Mountains. Meinig has suggested that far western settlement and organization between the 1840s and 1870s spread outward from the six urban centers of Los Angeles, San Francisco, Portland, Salt Lake City, Denver, and Santa Fe. We can easily add Galveston and San Antonio (with its commercial dominance of the south Texas cattle trade and the developing agricultural regions of the Hill Country). Secondary islands of settlement centered on Helena, Boise, Phoenix, and El Paso. As railroad builders added more links to the western transportation system in the 1880s and 1890s, the isolated metropolitan regions merged into the national hierarchy of cities focused on New York and Chicago. At the peak of the industrial era in the 1920s, economist N.S.B. Gras and sociologist Robert Park could both summarize the West as a set of twelve or fourteen metropolitan regions that connected farming market centers and mining towns to the national capitals of commerce.[20] Although San Antonio remained the largest city in Texas and the seventh largest in the West as late as 1920, for example, its prosperity and its hinterland depended upon the city's linkages to national markets.[21]

Cities of the second urban revolution were, above all, modern. Their leaders were eager to adapt new technologies and institutions. Houston's commercial elite built an infrastructure of public services in direct imitation of northeastern cities. Western cities eagerly adopted the latest techniques and approaches to city planning and displayed their respectable maturity by catering to tourists, hosting political conventions (as with Denver's Democratic Convention in 1904), and staging world's fairs (as in Portland, Seattle, San Diego, and San Francisco between 1905 and 1915). They imitated New York and Chicago by erecting sets of cut-down skyscrapers in the 1910s and 1920s.[22] The modernization of western cities was a regional version of the transformation of the Atlantic capitals as the second urban revolution worked its way to a climax. London's transformation from the dark and mysterious city of Dickens into an imperial metropolis and Baron Haussmann's efforts to make Paris safe for railroads and department stores were mirrored in smaller compass in the establishment of city and regional park systems and civic centers for cities like Denver and San Francisco. When Herbert Croly visited Portland in 1912, he found a mature and cultured (and self-satisfied) city whose solid and dignified "business structures are as good . . . as the average of those erected in the Middle West or in the East."[23]

Modern also meant socially diverse. Western cities lacked the massive immigrant communities of a New York or Cleveland, but each of the metropolitan centers had recognizable ethnic neighborhoods by the turn of the century. Scandinavians filled Seattle's Ballard district, Italians moved into San Francisco's North Beach, and Slavic immigrants filled Denver's Globeville. Chinese communities in Seattle, Tacoma, Portland, and San Francisco drew the greatest attention from tourists in search of the exotic; local reformers worried about opium dens and anti-Oriental mobs.

At the same time, of course, western cities were provincial by definition. They were conduits for eastern investment in ranches, copper mines, smelters, and shingle mills.[24] They were simultaneously consumers of metropolitan culture in the form of traveling theater troupes, musicians, and lectures. On occasion they were keepers of regional identity and culture. Californians consciously constructed urban identities to define the character of their new society. Salt Lake City remained the capital of a distinctive cultural region into the later twentieth century.[25]

The pace of development slowed after 1893 and ground nearly to a halt by the 1920s outside the petroleum states. The rate of urbanization tracked that of the United States after outpacing it for half a century. The regional pause resulted from a shift in the focus of industrial growth to new high-technology industries such as chemicals and electrical equipment that were best developed out of the industrial and educational base of the Northeast. Primary industries found it hard to compete against General Motors or Westinghouse for attention or investment.[26]

Although the West was parceled and organized through its cities at the turn of the twentieth century, much of its daily life in the farming and ranching districts remained isolated from urban influences. The day-to-day isolation of the hinterlands exacerbated the effects of the long economic pause and allowed state and regional politics to revolve around provincial revolts against the industrial cores. The political consequence was a series of ultimately unsuccessful regional revolts that tried and failed to create effective alternatives to national capitalism or to establish significant freedom action for local communities—the Farmers Alliance and Populist politics of Texas and the central plains in the 1880s and 1890s; the Western Federation of Miners in the Rockies in the 1890s; homegrown socialism in states like Oklahoma; and the Industrial Workers of the World in the early twentieth century.[27] By the 1920s and 1930s, the protest had turned nostalgic rather than revolutionary. The Ku Klux Klan tapped the frustrations of Coloradans, Californians, Texans, Oklahomans, and Oregonians who found its attacks on foreigners and city-bred lifestyles the only convenient way to strike back at the increasing scale and complexity of American life.[28] The same frustrations that led carpenters and druggists to join the KKK also fueled bitter complaints from western intellectuals about the colonial captivity of their plundered province.[29]

After the regional stagnation and limited growth of the early twentieth century, the past half century has brought a transformation of western cities and the western urban system. As sociologist R. D. McKenzie commented in 1927, "In the course of time most frontiers grow up. They pass from a pioneer to a settled condition, and in turn become new centers of dominance."[30] Writing from the University of Washington, McKenzie was thinking both of the maturing of the United States vis-à-vis England and of Japan and the Orient vis-à-vis the Atlantic nations. The point is equally apt for the contrast between the dependency of the American West in the nineteenth century and its emergence as an independent source of economic and cultural change in the later twentieth century.

This transformation has involved the region's headlong participation in the world's third urban revolution. Patterns of global urbanization now reflect the instant mobility of capital in an unregulated world banking system, the emergence of newly industrialized nations of East Asia as part of the rich North, and the development of a networked world economy with a cluster of world cities and intricate international exchanges among second-level cities. Within the American West, patterns of urban-regional growth have reflected the new internationalization of the American economy, the global shift toward services (especially those involved in the leisure economy of recreation and retirement), and the expansion of the garrison state as a result of national policy decisions. Expanded multilateral ties to the nation and world in cities like Seattle, Dallas, and San Diego are a substantial step beyond the metropolitan regions of Gras and Meinig.[31]

We can read the new trends in the transformation of San Antonio from a sleepy regional city to a sophisticated metropolis. Most obviously, the city grew with the army and air force from 1940 to 1990. Defense-related businesses ranged from government contractors (as had been true since the nineteenth century) to the United Services Automobile Association providing auto insurance to active and retired military and their dependents. Leisure industries range from military retirees to a booming convention business supported by the lucky accident of the Riverwalk, a new convention center, and a downtown festival market. The 1980s also brought efforts to expand medical and high technology businesses and to develop the city's communication infrastructure. Planned to coincide with the Mexico City Olympics of 1968, Hemisfair marked an official renewal of interest in trade with Latin America. More recently, Mayor Henry Cisneros defined an information-based growth strategy in an "Orange Book" report titled "San Antonio's Place in the Technology Environment," while other civic leaders have broached plans to make the city a Latin American banking and branch office center on the model of Miami.[32]

San Antonio's openings to Latin America are a few steps short of development as a genuine "world city." Over the past thirty years, the growing ease of instant communication has allowed centralization of international finance, corporate headquarters, and business services in a handful of cities—New York, London, and Tokyo, supported by Paris, São Paulo, Hong Kong, Singapore, and Los Angeles. A notch below are cities like San Francisco, Dallas, Houston, and Honolulu with extensive international connections as measured by direct overseas flights, foreign banking offices, foreign investment, exports and imports, immigrants, and tourists.[33]

Centralization of economic control has been accompanied by a revolutionary restructuring of the metropolitan fabric. Western cities have experienced the galloping Manhattanization of their downtown office cores *along with* radical decentralization. The North Side of San Antonio, with its clusters of commercial development around the airport and the South Texas Medical Center, illustrates the proliferation of edge cities. The same decentralization of business has restructured the Bay Area, Houston, Dallas, and Phoenix. Super suburbs like Aurora, Anaheim, Arlington, and Bellevue compete directly with older city centers.[34]

Beyond the fringe of western exurbs, the urban system model recognizes the steady reduction of rural isolation. The western heartlands—Snake River Valley, Montana plains, San Juan Mountains of Colorado, Utah Canyonlands—were non-Europeanized in the eighteenth century. They were the hinterlands of a new system of cities in the nineteenth century. They have been embraced within urban recreation, commuting, and amenity zones in the later twentieth. This extraordinary penetration of the empty West by the urban West involves the appropriation of natural resources for new purposes—grazing land for garbage disposal and nuclear waste, forests for scenic preservation, farming districts for sources of water. The changes have brought deep conflicts over environmental change, perhaps most notoriously in the case of the Owens Valley.[35]

Tensions between urban realities and rural imagery are reflected in regional literature. Essayists chronicle the work of geologists and naturalists as the modern equivalents of miners and mountain men. Regional novelists choose their contemporary protagonists from ranchers, farmers, loggers, rodeo riders, and river rafters. Their topics are Native Americans, nature, and life in the land of wind and storm.[36] At the same time, perceptive writers embed rural characters in the urban system. Williston and Fargo offer the lure of bright lights for the rural families in Louise Erdrich's *Love Medicine.* The folks of Larry McMurtry's west Texas town of Thalia drive to Oklahoma City for disco and to Dallas to consult a doctor.[37]

Indeed, the importance of cities as inspiration for western writers is obscured by the tendency to recognize as "western" only those artists who deal with small towns and open landscapes. Wallace Stegner and Ivan Doig are "western" writers but Maxine Hong Kingston is an ethnic or feminist writer. Ross McDonald and Raymond Chandler are genre novelists, not regionalists. Thomas Pynchon, Joan Didion, and Alison Lurie are "mainstream." Larry McMurtry is western when his topic is a nineteenth-century cattle drive but not when he writes about contemporary Houston or Las Vegas. Literary histories remember Walter Van Tilburg Clark's stories about nineteenth-century westerners far more often than his novel about twentieth-century Reno.[38]

The same contrast is summarized by the public response to two painters who came to the Southwest as outsiders and remained to be captivated by the clarity of southwestern light. Englishman David Hockney's reaction to Los Angeles in the 1960s was a series of stunning depictions of the lawn sprinklers, high-rise buildings, and swimming pools of Santa Monica, Hollywood, and Beverly Hills. The surfaces glare and stare back at the viewer in the "technicolor daylight" of California. The clear light of New Mexico similarly drew easterner Georgia O'Keefe to paint and repaint the sun-bleached skulls of cattle. The international art world has recognized and applauded Hockney's urban and suburban imagery. The middlebrow public in the United States has adopted O'Keefe's traditionally regional subject as a national icon. As with literature, Americans prefer to neglect the urban West and to admire what they know to be comfortably western.

Urban Systems and the Historiography of the West

A city-centered approach to western history views the growth of urban settlements as the key process that has introduced "history" into the West in the form of continuous societal change. The urban outposts of the eighteenth century linked the West to a world of mercantile capitalism and competing empires of commerce. The urban-industrial revolution of the mid-nineteenth century created domestic equivalents of Lagos or Saigon—quasi-colonial gateways that mobilized regional resources and markets for the new world of industrial capitalism. The third urban system of the later twentieth century directly connects the West to national and global exchanges of goods, people, and information.

In describing the transformation of the West from a dependent frontier to a source region for economic and cultural change, an urban system model places regional development squarely within the larger realm of settlement history, a term that links the historical worlds of Bernard Bailyn, Oscar Handlin, Harold Innis, N.S.B. Gras, and David Potter.[39] Trans-Atlantic colonization, nineteenth-century immigration, the occupation of resource lands, and the construction of great industrial and commercial cities are all part of the same story of settlement. The history of the nation's western frontier becomes one contributing element to the larger process of repeopling and reconfiguring a continent.

As previously mentioned, the approach is clearly part of the "new" rather than the old western history. Even though Frederick Jackson Turner asked many of the right questions about the process of continental development, he looked too narrowly for the answers. Historians of western cities see continuities from the eighteenth century through the twentieth, find constant interactions between the West and the world, and expect to discover that cities were arenas that concentrated conflicts among groups and cultures. They are likely to follow Gene Gressley's suggestion to place the West firmly in the nation and the world.[40]

An urban system approach can be placed among three other interpretations that have dominated western regional history in recent decades. Historians who emphasize the interaction of landscape and culture look inward to find an essential and irreducible West. Historians who emphasize institutional continuity peer backward over the shoulders of the pioneers to search out the organizational and cultural hearths of western settlement. Students of comparative frontiers look sidewise to find comparable experiences in other nations. The urban historian is likely to find that the first approach tries to restate a western distinctiveness that never existed. The second and third approaches, in contrast, have important elements in common with an urban view.

In the first instance, an interpretation that emphasizes the systematic urbanization of the West also de-emphasizes the cultural consequences of the West's physical environment. From the early version of Walter Prescott Webb to the current ideas of Donald Worster, this interpretation understands the West as a different society because of the constraints and opportunities of its land and landscape.[41] It looks away from the urban West and the overwhelming majority of city-based westerners toward the wide open spaces. It searches for the unifying characteristics of a common regional core, usually finding the real West in resource production, arid lands, and empty space. Its undeniable aesthetic appeal leads our attention to the bright deserts and high mountains and invites historians to quote John Muir and Edward Abbey.

With every passing year, however, this approach defines away more and more westerners and more and more parts of the West. It is, in fact, a rationale for subregional history of the Rocky Mountain states and southern California, not for a larger western history. Resource production has been declining in relative importance to city-based manufacturing and service industries since the first decades of this century, even in Deep West states such as Idaho and Utah.[42] Aridity as a test of westernness excludes Austin, Dallas, Portland, Seattle, and wintertime Los Angeles, not to mention Hilo and Juneau. Space itself is of dubious meaning for a twentieth century in which the sources of regional change have been major cities and their far-reaching networks of communication and exchange.

In contrast, an urbanization model that highlights the integration of a settlement region into national and world economies necessarily describes the transplantation of economic and social institutions. Since Earl Pomeroy's classic essay "Continuity and Environment," historians have explored the westward migration of cultural forms as well as people. We have traced the recreation of political institutions, the reproduction of eastern value systems, and the consumption of eastern cultural products in successive Wests. Indeed, the economic and institutional incorporation of the West supplies some of the strongest evidence for Robert Wiebe's idea that the United States has moved from a federation of "island communities" in the nineteenth century to a national society in the twentieth century.[43]

In the same way, an urban interpretation places the development of the West comfortably within the powerful "organizational synthesis" of modern American history. That synthesis points to the increasing scale and complexity of organizations and institutional forms during the past century as a common theme among the often disparate experiences of government, corporations, and private associations.[44] The approach allows us to see the articulation of individual metropolitan regions and their connection through increasingly elaborate networks of migration, internal commerce, finance, and corporate control as elements of national organizational integration. The cities of the nineteenth-century West assiduously reproduced the forms of older eastern cities and built their economic institutions and corporations within the institutional space allowed by eastern and European investors. With the maturing of the urban West in the twentieth century, a complex trade in cultural forms has superseded a simple one-way transfer. Since World War II the Bay Area has nurtured and exported a vibrant literature, new life-styles, and new sets of political issues. California suburbs have become one of the prototypes for the modern American community. Disneyland, Sun City, and Silicon Valley are models for decentralizing cities from Florida to Massachusetts. Las Vegas is the model for Atlantic City and every other town that dreams of salvation through slot machines. Los Angeles is *the* test case for late twentieth-century urbanization.[45]

Finally, an analysis of urban systems dovetails with other work in comparative regional history by suggesting the value of dissolving "western" history as a separate category. As Patricia N. Limerick and others have argued, western history is part of American and world history, not a complete story in itself. Rather than looking inward to search out a shrinking western core, it may be more fruitful to look outward to understand the West as a continuing participant in a set of larger national, continental, or world regions.[46]

One such option for reorganizing our sense of regional history is to write the joint history of the American South and West as a single resource region that has undergone a transition from quasi-colonial periphery to urbanized Sunbelt over the past century. The South as well as the West found its development on hold from the 1890s to the 1930s.[47] During the economic cycle of 1890–1940, the cities of the industrial core controlled investment capital and set the limits for local commercial-civic elites. The new southern mill towns along the two slopes of the Appalachians were the regional equivalent of western lumber mill and smelter cities. Gastonia and Pueblo alike functioned within the tolerances of eastern corporations and markets. The same was true at a larger scale for Denver with its Guggenheim smelters and Birmingham with its U.S. Steel mills. The deflationary collapse of southern and western resource industries in the 1920s and 1930s accelerated the outmigration from wheat farms and cotton belt to regional cities. The reactive politics of the KKK found the same comfortable home in Atlanta and Knoxville as in Denver.

Since 1935, in contrast, much of the economic and military power of the nation has been mobilized to promote and develop the peripheral regions in a classic example of the liberal model of foreign aid. Federal spending on public works, rural modernization, shipbuilding, aircraft, atomic energy, and military bases inexorably altered the balance between rural and urban opportunities. The resulting migrations mingled the cultures of the Mississippi Valley and Southwest and made Bakersfield a second Little Rock or Nashville.[48] The transformation of the old periphery into a new core marked by increasingly independent cities was complete by the 1970s and 1980s, when popular commentary recognized the Sunbelt as a new region.[49] Multiracial immigration and the application of the Voting Rights Act to both Hispanic and African-American minorities have created common preconditions for metropolitan politics.[50] America of the third urban revolution is anchored simultaneously by Washington and Los Angeles, Atlanta and Dallas, Miami and Seattle. The forces of the defense economy, leisure economy, and internationalized economy have driven the cities of the South Atlantic and Gulf coasts as much as those of the Pacific coast. Miami is the mirror of Honolulu, Norfolk of San Diego, Knoxville of Albuquerque, Orlando of Anaheim.[51]

Historians uncomfortable with the reality of the Sunbelt might alternatively reconceptualize the history of the West as the story of two distinct regions pointed south toward Mexico and north toward Canada. The Greater Southwest can be approached in terms of Donald Meinig's description of cultural regions as consisting of cores, domains of substantial influence, and spheres of more attenuated influence.[52] The Mexamerican core is formed by the bi-national cities that line the border from San Diego/Tijuana to Brownsville/Matamoros. These bifurcated communities house nearly 5 million Americans and 3 million Mexicans. Their unified pools of consumers and workers are symbolized by the rise of the *maquila* factories in Mexico.[53]

In a larger geographic framework, the five states of the Southwest counted twenty-five metropolitan areas with at least 50,000 Hispanic residents in 1980. "Spanish" Santa Fe and Tucson balance the "midwestern" cities of Albuquerque and Phoenix. East Los Angeles and westside San Antonio have served as staging grounds for Mexican immigration and centers for Mexican-American institutions for several generations. The sphere of the Greater Southwest has pushed northward with the permanent settlement of Hispanic farm workers. The boundary can be marked by the location of communities in which Mexican-born residents outnumbered Canadian-born. In 1950, the line ran between San Jose and San Francisco, Pueblo and Denver, Topeka and Omaha. By 1980, Omaha, Denver, Casper, Reno, San Francisco, Portland, Yakima, and Richland had been annexed to the fringes of

Latin America. In the realm of popular culture, this sphere roughly coincides with the area in which Mexican restaurants outnumber Chinese and Italian restaurants as the most common "ethnic" eateries.[54]

The Greater Southwest is layered historically as well as spatially. A nineteenth-century zone of cross-border banditry and contests for control of local communities has become the twentieth-century's core commuting region. The first urban system of the eighteenth century defined the boundaries of the larger Southwest. Studies of the urbanization of Hispanic populations over multiple generations within the Mexican-American domain constitute some of the most interesting of recent western scholarship.[55]

The similarities of Canadian and U.S. culture and populations have made the Greater Northwest less obvious than the Greater Southwest. As late as 1980, however, Canada remained the most important source of immigrants for Billings, Bismarck, Great Falls, Spokane, Provo, Medford, and Redding. Although the common histories of western Canada and the western United States have often been treated in terms of comparative frontiers, it is equally valuable to look at common patterns of urban development. Vancouver, Seattle, and Portland share such remarkable similarities in economic base and urban style that Seattle's *New Pacific* magazine took on the cause that "Cascadia" is a single economic and social region inconveniently divided by a political border. Edmonton, Calgary, Denver, Oklahoma City, Dallas, and Houston are all parts of a mid-continental energy empire. Winnipeg ("where the New West begins") has been as much a gateway to the Great Plains as Minneapolis, Omaha, or Kansas City.[56]

The same trade in furs that created a Greater Northwest also tied the West to the world of the Pacific Ocean. The Anglo-American ranchers in a district like eastern Oregon are actually latecomers, retracing the footsteps of Chinese miners from the 1860s and the Hawaiian employees of the Hudson Bay Company who gave their name to the Owyhee River in the 1820s. Chinese immigrants were the largest ethnic group in San Francisco, Portland, and Seattle by 1880. A century later, Asians outnumbered both Hispanics and Canadians in thirty-five metropolitan areas. New migrations since 1960 have added Filipinos, Vietnamese, Koreans, Samoans, and other Pacific nationalities to long-established Chinese and Japanese communities.

In an intriguing example of the possibilities of Pacific urban history, Australian economist Lionel Frost has suggested that the younger settlement regions of western Canada, the western United States, Australia, and New Zealand produced a common type of city in the later nineteenth century. His analysis distinguishes between Atlantic cities (industrial centers of the second urban revolution plus the capitals of Australia's original convict colonies) and cities of a "new urban frontier." The former were dense and crowded, the latter loose and sprawling, using available land to house the majority of their residents in single-family houses rather than teeming tenements. In a reversal of the frequent argument about quasi-colonial cities, he argues that the commercial cities of the new urban frontier had few manufacturing opportunities to divert local capital from housing and utilities.[57]

To a substantial extent, the West's Pacific turn of the mid-twentieth century has resulted from the creation of a metropolitan-military complex during the three Pacific wars of 1940–1945, 1950–1953, and 1962–1974. San Diego, San Francisco, Seattle, and Honolulu were the last stops before Asian bases and Indochinese battle zones. Decisions to support the indefinite projection of American power into the western Pacific and to manage continental defense through nuclear deterrence pointed the West toward East Asia and Siberia. Supply and training bases, shipyards, and aircraft maintenance facilities around Seattle-Tacoma, Salt Lake City, San Antonio, Oklahoma City, San Diego, and San Francisco supported forward bases in the Philippines, Korea, Guam, and Japan. NORAD in Colorado Springs and SAC in Omaha shared command and control. Minuteman bases were supervised from Cheyenne and Great Falls and depended on Distant Early Warning radars managed from Fairbanks and Anchorage.

Historical perspective also reminds us that the vast expansion of trans-Pacific trade in the 1970s and 1980s is the realization of ambitions that date to the opening of the century, when West Coast cities turned their eyes to the possibilities of Asian markets. American victory in World War II reconfirmed the desire of cities like San Francisco to "benefit as a focal point for increased trade with hitherto underdeveloped countries in the Pacific Basin and South America."[58] Pacific trade and immigration have transformed Los Angeles into a global city that has shadowed but not undermined San Francisco's role as a second center of international banking, professional services, and multinational corporate headquarters. Historians of the Pacific Rim can also explore the internationalization of second-level cities like Seattle, San Diego, Dallas, Houston. Especially interesting is the neglected case of Honolulu, a would-be Vienna of the Pacific whose global connections were pioneered by the importation of Asian workers in the early twentieth century, reconfirmed when its big corporations diversified into manufacturing and construction throughout the Pacific basin, and reinforced by Japanese tourists, hotel builders, and investors looking for second homes.[59]

The Urban West: Between the Frontier and the World

Every historian of the West knows the symbolic meaning of the census of 1890, when federal officials declared that it was no longer possible to find a distinct frontier line on the map of the United States. The equally important statement that "the urban element in the Western division . . . has gained somewhat more rapidly than the total population" attracted less attention. In fact, the level of urbanization in the Rocky Mountain and Pacific states (30 percent) had already passed that for the country as a whole (28 percent) by the census of 1880.

At the end of the twentieth century, the West is inescapably urban. To find nineteen of the nation's twenty-five fastest growing metropolitan areas, Americans in the 1940s had to cross the Missouri or Sabine rivers into the western half of the nation. The same western states counted sixteen of the twenty-five fastest growing metropolitan areas during the 1950s, thirteen during the 1960s, sixteen for the 1970s, and fifteen for 1980–1988. Urban growth was felt at all levels of the urban system. Between 1940 and 1990, Phoenix moved from ninety-first place to twentieth among American metropolitan areas. San Diego from fiftieth to fifteenth, and Dallas from thirty-first to ninth. The dozen largest western metropolitan areas (as of 1990) accounted for 28 percent of *all* of the population increase in the United States between 1940 and 1990 and for 36 percent for the 1980s.

The western metropolitan frontier that is summarized in these statistics has connected the old resource West to the world of the late twentieth century. The Burlington Northern Railroad still sends its trains rumbling along the edge of downtown Billings on a line that first opened in 1882. Quiet neighborhoods climb from the Yellowstone River to the base of the rimrock. When local businesspeople fill downtown restaurants to pack away breakfast and talk land, insurance, and hunting, it could still be 1925. Look a little more deeply, however, and Billings owes its new airport, its rehabbed hotels, and its midrise office buildings to its role in the world energy business. When residents turn out by the thousands at Cobb Field to watch the Billings Mustangs of the Pioneer League, they're not cheering for local heros but for Ohioans and Venezuelans. The visiting teams from Pocatello and Medicine Hat have their own shares of New Yorkers, Floridians, and Latin Americans.

The metropolitan frontier has also helped to connect the United States to the world outside its borders. Cities like Los Angeles, Seattle, Honolulu, and San Antonio represent the American future as a multiethnic nation. Eastern cities from the 1840s to the 1940s struggled to adapt the narrow culture of North Sea Protestantism to the full range of European languages, religions, and national loyalties. The cities of the West and Southwest have had to blend a much wider range of European Americans, African Americans, Latin Americans, and

Asian Americans. In the process, they have been the arenas in which one of the hidden themes of the American frontier has been most fully played out. In the 1860s or 1870s, Anglo-Americans, Mexicans, and Chinese met everywhere across the landscape—in railroad construction crews, in mining camps, and in cities from San Antonio to Tacoma. A century later, they mixed primarily in the West's booming cities. World War II and federal policies in the 1950s drew African-American migrants and pushed Native Americans into Phoenix, Los Angeles, Seattle, and Denver. The renewed international migrations after 1965 also targeted the urban West.

One way to visualize the changing character of the modern West is to visit downtown Los Angeles. To walk from Main Street to the Harbor Freeway is to cross a series of divides between the past and future of western cities. The retail and entertainment core from the 1920s and 1930s along Broadway and Spring streets has now become the downtown for Hispanic East Los Angeles. Its sidewalks at 5:00 P.M. are crowded with Latino and Asian immigrants waiting for southbound and eastbound buses. Many new westerners earn their living in the garment district east of Main Street, whose shops and factories have been kept open in the 1980s by the cheap labor of legal and illegal immigrants. Six blocks further west is the new upscale city of "L.A. Law" where accountants and bankers swing out of subsurface parking garages onto westbound freeways. The old downtown was built with domestic capital to serve southern California consumers, farmers, and oilmen. The new downtown is increasingly controlled by overseas investors and serves the trading needs of the industrialized Pacific Rim. The downtown Los Angeles of 1940, with its loft buildings and Art Deco facades, is Billings writ large. Both the sleek, self-satisfied, retail-office complexes that cluster along the Harbor Freeway and sport the names of overseas banks and the Broadway movie marquees that announce movies made in Mexico are harbingers of a probable multiethnic and international future of the next century.

DONALD WORSTER

Rediscovering the West: The Legacy of John Wesley Powell

Understanding the western past must always begin with understanding the land itself, or what today we ambiguously call "the environment." By land I mean a composite of biophysical forces, living and nonliving, including climate, geology, flora, and fauna functioning together over time. Leave those entangled forces out of the story, and the human characters themselves become quite unrecognizable. Crazy Horse is not the same man if we extract him from his natural surroundings and transport him to a Polish forest. Even the invading whites become unfamiliar if we leave out their experiences with the land: the gold-bearing mountain streams, the bison and pronghorn fleeing from their guns, or the view out the windshield of an aging jalopy. The West has not been an empty stage on which a cast of characters assembled to talk among themselves. It has been a powerful landscape that has entered into the drama at every point, shaping the dialogue. Western historians who ignore that landscape are like censors who have left the dialogue full of blanks and the meaning gone.

Westward-moving pioneers, creaking along the Oregon and Santa Fe trails of the last century, understood the importance of the landscape with a vividness that a scholar today might have to struggle to imagine. They came into a country of raw physical nature, less mediated by the forces of life than the eastern side of the continent. The sheltering forests thinned out, then disappeared over most of the terrain. The earth lay before the traveler like a massive brown body, every crevice, bulge, and scar from the past relentlessly revealed. The landscape was larger than the eye could take in and more uncovered than a modest rural family could feel comfortable with. Even the grass was too short and sparse to shelter them from cosmic eyes.

Of course, as farmers they had seen cleared-off lands before and were familiar with the earth's anatomy. But beyond the Missouri River the landscape was shockingly bare. It was not a cleared space at all, shaped and controlled by human labor and softened by human habitation or even by vegetation. It was a landscape starkly expressing the power of the inorganic: an overpowering sky, swift-moving clouds, wide-swinging rivers, rugged buttes and mountains, vast desiccated plains, all expressions of geophysical forces that completely dominated the kingdom of plants and animals. The pioneer endured some of the world's driest deserts, fixed in the hard grip of upper atmospheric wind currents that pulled water vapor from the distant Pacific Ocean, dropped it in the high Sierras and Rockies, leaving the low-lying lands between parched and deadly. This elemental landscape presented an altogether new kind of wildness to the pioneer, beyond European or eastern American experience, which had long been focused on a struggle to create farms out of forests. This was a wildness of sunlight and shadow, heat and cold, sandstone and granite.

The western land was not only big, brown, bare, and imposing; it also confronted the traveler with a time-scale that was older than anyone had once supposed possible. The many species of plants and animals, scientists had begun to realize by the early nineteenth century, had existed long before 4004 B.C., which was the year Archbishop James Ussher had calculated was the year of creation; bones dug from the ground proved how wrong he was. But the earth itself was far, far older than any kind of animal fossil. Scientists had begun talking about an ancient Devonian time, a Cambrian period of history, a Precambrian period, and closer to the present, a Carboniferous, a Triassic, a Jurassic, a Cretaceous period. Life had appeared only in the later phases of that history. This was a revolutionary chronology.

A western traveler familiar with those scientific developments, and surely there were a few such among the hundreds of thousands that went west, had to realize that this new country was not new at all. They were traveling back in time as well as forward to opportunity. From a wagon seat a pioneer looked out on plains of loess blown in at the end of last Ice Age. She peered into canyons cut through layers of rock deposited in the unimaginable eras of the past; faced mountains uplifted by tectonic powers that we have begun to understand only in past few decades; passed over hidden seas and rivers buried hundreds of feet underground, their signature written in gravel and limestone beds that only modern deep-drilling rigs can actually touch, that no human will ever see. Today, we have fixed precise dates for those landscapes running back millions of years into the past. No pioneer could have grasped just how immensely old the western land really was. But surely a few must have sensed now and then that they had entered a place where time extended before any civilization anywhere had appeared. They must have sensed, whatever their scientific training, that living organisms, and human communities too, had been highly vulnerable to those mighty physical elements. The age of the great trek westward was also an age beginning to discover deep time, on a scientific and on a popular level, time beyond the mythology of Genesis. As a result, those very humans were about to be displaced from the center of creation.

Among the many Americans who looked with intense interest and expectation toward the opening of the West was John Wesley Powell of Bloomington, Illinois. Anyone who seeks to understand the West as environment and its implications for human history must begin by remembering Powell and following the process of his education. He first read about the western land from that rambling military man, John Charles Frémont, author of the *Report of the Exploring Expedition to the Rocky Mountains in the Year 1842*. Eventually he talked with Frémont and corresponded with scientists about western natural history. Increasingly bored with his life as a classroom teacher, Powell itched to be out among those magnificent rocks.

In summer 1867, Wes Powell was at last on his way west, guiding a group of undergraduate students and small-town amateur naturalists over the rutted plains along the Platte River, the route of pioneers. They passed wagon trains filled with rural folk looking for productive homesteads. Powell, however, was heading in a different direction: to the Badlands of Dakota, where the White River has cut deeply into fine white clay sediments intermixed with thin sandstone layers, a place no farmer could love. Powell must have seen in such a sterile but strangely beautiful place the possibilities of a good crop of scientific discovery. But at Fort Laramie, discouraged by reports of growing Indian resistance to white expeditions, the travelers changed their minds and turned south into Colorado, heading for Pike's Peak. It was a momentous adjustment of course, for during that summer in the Colorado high country, Powell first heard about the unexplored reaches of the Colorado River, where erosion had worked on the grandest scale anywhere, where the river was reputed to disappear into vast subterranean conduits, where waterfalls larger than any ever seen by humans might thunder. What had begun as a college outing abruptly led to a new ambition: to explore that fabled river through its canyons, whatever the risk, and add dramatic new knowledge to the American mind.

In late May 1869, at one o'clock in the afternoon on the Green River, Powell and nine other men set off downstream on the mission that would make his name great. Had the Sioux been a little less resistant to interlopers, he might have been digging away in the Badlands or clambering around the Black Hills before Custer got there and discovered gold. Instead, by the workings of circumstance and ambition, he and a remnant five of his men loaded into two little boats became the first Americans to navigate successfully the shadowed, dangerous labyrinth of the Colorado canyonlands. They came out of the labyrinth on August 30 at Grand Wash Cliffs, and Powell returned to the settlements a national hero.

In that decade of the 1860s the American West began to emerge for the first time as a distinctive region of the country. For a long while it had been as mysteriously located as heaven or hell. "West" referred to a compass direction, a general trend of movement, a fantasy land rather than to a particular place with a particular past. As a study in popular mythology that older, vaguer West was highly interesting, but it lacked concreteness and defied reliable knowledge. After the Civil War, however, the vagueness began to disappear and for the first time the West took shape as a distinctive new region of the United States.

The nation had some prior experience with regionalism, though little of it good. During Powell's growing-up years many local loyalties in America, dating from colonial days, had been replaced by a rising nationalism; yet in those same years a common national identity had increasingly been thwarted by the growing confrontation of North against South. In the North people had become Yankees all, from Lawrence, Massachusetts, to Lawrence, Kansas, while in the slave-owning and -trading South they had developed a strong sense of being different. We may call that complex process of fusion and fission by the name of sectionalism, which was the nineteenth-century term for departures from a single national identity, or we may call it regionalism, a twentieth-century term; but the process was one and the same. By 1861 Americans had created two major ways of being American, based on disparities of environment, labor, race, and tradition, but then found they could not tolerate those differences. They fell into a war when the North tried to impose its definition of Americanness on the South, a war that left both regions bloodied and exhausted. Together, the North and the South had made a botch of the Founding Fathers' dreams of a new unified civilization.

Had the re–United States in 1865 been forced to live within the confines of its old territory, the North and the South might still be nursing old grudges, always ready to divide and fight again, like the Czechs and Slovaks, the Serbs and Croats. But fortunately that was not to be; they had a vast expense of land stretching westward from the Great Plains to the Pacific Coast that diverted their attention. All of that land was under American ownership. What could be made of it? How might it heal a wounded civilization?

They called that great space the West—the part of the country where the passions of the Civil War had been less bitterly felt, the battlefields had been fewer, the old rivalries less rooted and intense. The West was wherever the North and South faded away. Its borders were still a little vague, of course, as regions always are, and the indefiniteness would persist for a long while as settlers brought into the West their old identities, their bitterness, their tattered uniforms and rusty wartime weapons. All the same, they came in a spirit of forgetting the failure of the war. The West would be neither North nor South, but a new, third way of being American. At the same time it would offer the promise of a new national unity, a new geography of hope, and a fresh beginning for a bankrupt nation.

Wes Powell was painfully aware of what the country had just been through. He had grown up in an abolitionist family and enlisted to fight as a private in the Illinois volunteer infantry before the war had begun. A year later, he was a company officer at the battle of Shiloh, Tennessee, when a minié ball struck him on the right arm, breaking the bones and embedding itself in the flesh so deeply it could not be removed. A druggist become war surgeon amputated his arm just above the elbow. For the rest of his life Powell would suffer frequent, intense pain in the stump of that arm, reminding him again and again of those fierce battlefields, the heavy smell of gunsmoke, the groans of other wounded men lying in hospital beds. But maimed though he was, he had gone back to the war, leaving the army only in 1865, with the rank of major. Four years later he went down the Colorado River, tied to a chair on the boat deck, the stump still throbbing, the trauma of sectional conflict a long way away but never to be forgotten. With others of his generation, he would seek a West beyond fratricide, at once familiarly nationalistic in its ambitions yet a distinctly better regionalism than all that gone before.

Today, John Wesley Powell's name is widely connected with the West, but what was his true significance for its development? In much of the popular literature he appears as a romantic adventurer, little different from Frémont or Kit Carson. He was the last in a line of hero-explorers, we are told, who revealed the way west and opened up the country for American expansion; he was an agent of imperialism who helped "win" the West, handing it over to a grateful nation, then abruptly disappearing.[1] Other interpretations of Powell bring him into the twentieth century, but what did he contribute to the region as we know it today? In the institutional memories of several federal agencies, such as the Geological Survey and the Bureau of Reclamation, Powell appears as the inspiration behind their growth and presence in the region.[2] Most western historians go beyond such characterizations and describe Powell as an important social reformer, but all they usually mean is that he tried to increase the size of agricultural land holdings allowed under the government's homestead laws in response to the western climate.

Despite several good biographies of the man, and a thousand brief acknowledgments of his importance, Powell remains widely misunderstood. He is everybody's hero, the intrepid pathfinder of the West's most charismatic river, a paragon of rational, scientific planning, and so forth. But his most significant legacy remains obscure and even forgotten. That legacy was a set of ideas pertaining to the American people's relationship to the western environment, ideas that were more radical, more sweeping than we have appreciated or ever tried to apply.

But before examining those ideas, we must understand their background and trace the stages of Powell's education in the western landscape. It was an education obtained in the field, not the library, as almost all his education had been, and it focused on the land itself, as I am suggesting the education of western historians ought to do.

Powell, as I have indicated, was a scientist interested in such topics as geology, geomorphology, stream hydraulics, and climate. He was not really engaged by biology of any sort; the native grasses he trod on in going west, the stunning wildlife he saw, the new ideas of biological evolution floating in the air did not really interest him. What seized his imagination was the inorganic. He sensed a compelling story in that realm, one that would reveal how the West had come to be what it was and would suggest to Americans what they needed to do if they were to make a successful civilization in the region. The western lands were not a blank slate on which any identity, old or new, could be arbitrarily written. One had to study what had occurred there before culture—any culture, Indian or European—had arrived. It was as a scientist, therefore, that Powell approached the latent region spreading out before him, and it is as a scientist that he speaks to us today, suggesting a history that incorporates the insights of the natural sciences gathered in the field.

Heretofore, regions had emerged from a long folk process of settling, gaining experience, adapting to the terrain. That was so in Europe and Asia as it was in North America. Both the North and the South of the United States had emerged before modern science had much influence over the popular mind, before the word scientist had even been coined. The American West would be different because it would take form in an age more deeply shaped by science and would owe much of its identity to the work of scientists like Powell.

Regions, to be sure, are based on something more than scientific definitions, even in the modern age. Other people came into the country too, people with no interest in science, and they were far more numerous than the explorer-scientists; there were entrepreneurs, rural settlers, laborers, women as well as men, people of all races, people from every corner of the earth. All of them contributed to the meaning of the West; consequently, the region would never have a single comprehensive identity. Despite Powell's hope, there is no single place to stand and take in the whole picture of so many diverse human beings. Western history is rightly understood as requiring us to see the place from every angle of vision.

But the diverse peoples of the West have had something in common too: a big, concrete physical landscape of rock, vapor, climate, and all its patterns of structure and process. A region may acquire many cultural meanings, as this one has, but it also has physical realities that provide a unifying experience and a shared set of historical challenges.

What made this region strikingly different from the eastern part of the country, Powell concluded, was its aridity. "The eastern portion of the United States," he wrote, "is supplied with abundant rainfall for agricultural purposes, receiving the necessary amount from the evaporation of the Atlantic Ocean and the Gulf of Mexico; but westward the amount of aqueous precipitation diminishes in a general way until at last a region is reached where the climate is so arid that agriculture is not successful without irrigation."[3] Powell based this generalization not only on his own observations but also on a rain chart compiled in 1868 for the Smithsonian Institution by Charles A. Shott, which showed that, aside from a humid coastal strip north of San Francisco toward Seattle and a few high mountain slopes, the West received less than twenty inches of rainfall a year on average.[4] The chart also showed that a broad belt separated the arid country from the eastern humid region—a "subhumid" belt that covered most of Texas, Oklahoma, Kansas, and Nebraska, "a beautiful prairie country throughout." It was the ecological threshold for the West, covering ten percent of the present entire United States exclusive of Alaska. The arid zone of the West was much larger still: forty percent of the entire country. So altogether the two major zones of the West covered a space that was quite as big as the East, beckoning to settlers tired of war, eager for land of their own, but confronting them with a colossal set of differences. The West would set rigorous new terms for their institutions and traditions.

The sinuous isohyetals on the Smithsonian chart must be seen by historians as at once natural and cultural facts. The cultural element began with agriculture. People invented agriculture when they chose some plants to eat, cultivating and breeding them, while ignoring others. That was so of all the major foods on which humans have depended: wheat, sugar, corn, rice, and so forth have all been cultural constructions. But food is also plant and animal life, and as such it is a part of nature. Food must fill the body's physiological needs. The West, the isohyetals suggested, could not fill those needs over much of its extent; it did not have enough moisture. Beyond a few oases, all of the foods cultivated by people anywhere on earth would have difficulty surviving there. That was a natural fact, and no amount of dreaming or experimenting could alter it. If people adapted their agricultural techniques and learned to raise food in those oases, they could manage to live comfortably. Nature, in any case, set the conditions for their success, and humans had no choice but to accept them.

As a scientist, impressed with the power of nature, Powell was to a point an environmental determinist: he assumed that any settlement of the region would be impossible without relying on agriculture as its core economic activity. He understood that nature determined, and had always determined, the essential style and scope of that agriculture. Unless Americans suddenly learned how to domesticate the native vegetation of the new region—sagebrush, Mormon tea, shadscale, cactus—and to eat their products, they were going to have to adapt.

Despite thousands of years of residence and much intelligent trial-and-error experimentation, the Indians had not still turned those native western plants into major foodstuffs, but had continued to rely on maize, pumpkins, and beans introduced from other parts of the hemisphere. Even so, they found they could cultivate them in only a few favorable locations. One might argue that they had been shaped by their cultural heritage as much by nature's patterns of aridity, but to make that argument would be to assume that plant domestication is a completely open possibility. In fact, domestication is always the outcome of a limited intelligence working on the limited possibilities afforded by plant and animal genetics. Powell did not reason all those matters out, but he did know, as any scientist must, that nature sets real, firm demands on the human species, so vitally dependent on water, protein, and minerals for its survival. That was knowledge, however, that many other Americans had not yet acquired, and that some historians still continue to ignore.

If Powell found the unifying environmental reality of the West in aridity, he also came to understand the economic realities that were sweeping into the West, as they were sweeping across the entire nation, in the 1870s. Men of wealth and power were everywhere looking for resources to exploit, putting into their private pockets as much as they could grasp.

They were claiming railroad rights-of-way, mineral deposits, timber stands, all the grasslands in the public domain, and most critical for the long-term development of the West, the scarce water resources. Other Americans who lacked means or avidity or shrewdness were quickly being shut out of the picture. Powell sensed that the new region would not belong to the common people if economic trends persisted. "If in the eagerness for present development," he warned, "a land and water system shall grow up in which the practical control of agriculture shall fall into the hands of water companies, evils will result therefrom that generations may not be able to correct, and the very men who are now lauded as benefactors to the country will, in the ungovernable reaction which is sure to come, be denounced as oppressors of the people."[5] Here is another idea that western history must always come back to—the idea that the past, like the present, has been largely a conflict over which group or class of individuals would gather the region's natural resources into its possession.

If science could reveal the structure of the natural environment, perhaps it could also suggest a better social order for the region. Powell's *Report on the Lands of the Arid Region,* published in 1878, provided a preliminary sketch of that social order. A familiar document to most western historians, its central theme is that the Ordinance of 1785 had to be scrapped, along with the whole system of transferring the public domain to private ownership. The ordinance had established a national land survey, the township-and-range system, that divided the country from the Appalachian Mountains to the Pacific Coast into a rigid grid of square parcels 1 mile on a side, subdivided into quarter sections of 160 acres. Scientific though it once had seemed in its geometrical precision, it disregarded all evidence from the natural sciences about the diversity of the country. As the survey approached the subhumid, then the arid, region, it would prove more and more inadequate. Settlers who selected a homestead from that grid might find themselves living on a barren mesa with no surface water at all or, conversely, locating on a well-watered, well-wooded bottomland with more acres than they could cultivate.

The rest of Powell's recommendations are also rather well known. He would scrap the entire body of homestead and preemption legislation and allow only two types of private land tenure in the West: small irrigated farms no larger than 80 acres, gathered together into irrigation districts; and large "pasturage farms," or livestock ranches, no larger than 2,560 acres, likewise organized into grazing districts. All other lands would remain in federal ownership, though the timber or mineral resources on them might be sold or given to private interests. All the water would belong to those who owned the land; no one could control any water who did not possess an irrigated or pasturage farm. Instead of a monopoly over scarce resources exercised by a few capitalists, Powell envisioned a region permanently put into the hands of the rural many, bound together in a common body politic.

Powell published those reform proposals in 1878, but nothing came of them. He was not heeded by Congress or the public. The General Land Office continued to follow the ordinance system with its abstract approach to the land. The typical homestead patented under the system remained for a long while the standard eastern 160-acre parcel, though eventually that size was increased somewhat for stockraisers. All those facts are common knowledge among western historians and have been pointed out repeatedly. What has not been said is that following Powell's initial failure to get his ideas adopted, he worked them over into an even more radical shape. All during the 1880s, while serving as head of the Geological Survey, he continued to lobby, with dogged persistence, for his proposals. But more important, he made the proposals more sweeping, comprehensive, and systematic, until by 1890 he had arrived at a master plan for the West that has never been sufficiently understood.

In the early months of that year Major Powell ("professor" would suit him better, for he had never lost his didactic style) ran a seminar for politicians and the public on understanding the West. The House Select Committee on Irrigation of Arid Lands in the United States held hearings during February and March on a bill "to cede the arid lands to the States and Territories wherein they are situate and to provide for irrigation and protection of forest lands and pasture lands." As the foremost authority on those lands, Powell repeatedly came to testify, each time bringing new maps to place on the wall before the congressmen. He intended to teach them, valley by valley, the logic of the western landscape and to suggest how a whole new political structure might be based on that logic. So far as I know Powell's maps no longer exist, and historians must try to create them imaginatively in order to grasp the same ecological truths of the region.

His first map was of the Rio Grande River, from its headwaters in Colorado to El Paso, Texas. Then on another day he came with a map of the entire West, all 1,340,000 square miles of it; then a map of regional coal fields, of the major timberlands and the minor scrub forests (colored in contrasting shades of green), of the upper Arkansas River basin, of the Colorado River basin, of the Snake and the Bear, of—but there he ended abruptly, in the middle of March, indicating that he was prepared to discuss every watershed in the West but was afraid he might exhaust the committee's patience with his passion for details.[6]

He wanted them to know the country as he knew it, both from high up on the canyon rims and down on the river, and to understand its patterns of water, climate, and geology that had been interacting over so many eons. He wanted them to realize how little of the country could ever grow crops; at most there was water available for irrigating 100 million acres, a mere 1 out of 9 acres, and that would require a considerable investment in storage reservoirs, of which there were next to none in 1890. He wanted the men in the hearing room to appreciate the conflicts that were already brewing in those western valleys, as upstream developers diverted the water that downstream farmers had depended on, in the case of the Rio Grande Valley, for over a hundred years. Above all, he wanted them to see that all the natural resources of the West were connected into a single integrated whole, so that what was done to the mountain forests affected the lowland streams, and the lands without water were intricately related to those with water.

The Indians and Hispanos who had settled the country seemed to have understood that environmental interrelatedness, but the Anglos did not. They came as possessive individuals pursuing private dreams, trying to fence in their portion of the whole. They failed to see how their lives were related to the lives of their neighbors or how their lands depended on all the other lands in the vicinity. That, in a nutshell, was the central ecological problem of the West. The land had a complex unity that had evolved over time; however, the white settlers thought about the land as they thought about each other, in simplifying, fragmenting terms and, consequently, would come to grief. Whey that was so, and why environmental understanding was different for the different ethnic groups, remains one of the basic issues in western history.

Powell would create a completely new set of government units (to augment, not replace, the state and county governments) based on what he called "hydrographic basins," or watersheds, reaching from one divide to another. "My theory," he explained, "is to organize in the United States another unit of government for specific purposes, for agriculture by irrigation, for the protection of the forests which are being destroyed by fire, and for the utilization of the pasturage which can only be utilized in large bodies; that is, to create a great body of commonwealths. In the main these commonwealths would be like country communities in the States."[7]

Powell had plotted on his maps the outlines of 140 such units in the West, though he thought another 10 or so might be added, each of them approximately the size of 2 average counties. Within each unit a small part of the land would be private property, mainly the irrigated farms, but much would be communal lands—the dry grasslands and mountain forests. Title to them would remain in federal hands, but the local people would have the use of them and would make rules for their management. "If they want that timber destroyed, if they want to sell it, if they want to destroy it and wipe out irrigation, they are responsible for it, and let them do as they please."[8]

A few weeks after Powell finished his testimony before the House committee, *Century Magazine* published a series of three articles by him, presenting the same environmental analysis and political blueprint to the general public. In the last of them, "Institutions for the Arid Lands," Powell acknowledged that he had been influenced by Spanish settlements in the Southwest and by the Mormons of Utah, who had effectively communalized their natural resources. The beauty of those models, in his eyes, was that they put power in the hands of local communities. He emphatically rejected the alternative, already being debated, of giving the federal government active, centralized control over western resources. The government should not cede its lands to the states, he felt, but neither should it set up a national administration to guard the forests (it would soon become "a hotbed of corruption") nor an irrigation administration to finance water development. "I say to the Government: Hands off! Furnish the people with institutions of justice, and let them do the work for themselves."[9]

The Spanish and Mormon models demonstrated that local community control would, in the long run, do more to educate people in stewardship of the earth, prevent large disparities of wealth, and be more efficient and economical. But again, the vital element in those models was that they must subordinate the individual landowner to the decisions of the group. Local control must be truly communitarian.

In that same year of Professor Powell's seminar on the West, 1890, the Census Bureau announced the end of the frontier. The population of the seventeen western states and territories had reached 6,451,000, and the number of people was so large and they were so spread out that there was no longer a single discernible line of advancing settlement. The biggest city in the region was San Francisco, with 298,000 inhabitants, but there were other sizable urban centers, including Denver (107,000), Los Angeles (50,000), Salt Lake City (45,000), and Seattle (43,000).[10] As presented, his commonwealth idea had a decidedly rural bias in a region that was already urban and industrial to a degree, and fast becoming more so.[11]

The region would develop further in agricultural terms too, notwithstanding the census pronouncement on the frontier. Over the next three decades more land would be taken up by homesteaders than in the previous three decades. From that perspective Powell may not have been too late when it came to reforming agricultural institutions. But was he too late when he called for dividing the West into 140 or 150 *agrarian* commonwealths? That is a matter that historians have not yet really taken up.

In any case, why did the region move instead to a very different system of natural resource management, one dominated by a federal establishment composed of such agencies as the Forest Service and the Bureau of Land Management, exercising supervision over a vast federal domain? And why, on the other hand, has the region seen the rise of a counterestablishment of regional entrepreneurs perennially opposing those agencies and seeking to open the public domain to private enterprise? The post-Powell history of the West has been, to a very great degree, a story of that conflict over ownership, regulation, and access to the land; yet even now we have not yet written an adequate account of how that conflict has unfolded or of how it has been fought on the ground from state to state.

The record does not show that anyone in the nation expressed any positive interest in Powell's recommendations at the time he gave them, nor even that there was any serious critical response that might have raised hard questions and forced him to work out the problems he had overlooked. The House committee listened to him politely but took no action, and whatever response the *Century* articles got is not recorded for posterity. Apparently, from the lack of any contrary evidence, we can say that the nation did not give them much thought at all, perhaps because they flew in the face of well-established institutions and, more seriously, in the face of a national culture of individualism. Homesteaders continued to come looking for a piece of land they could manage on their own, while the powerful lobbies for western development, led by railroad corporations, mining companies, cattle outfits invading the public domain, and the like, could not have seen much merit in so many commonwealths getting in their way. Moreover, the conservationists, beginning with Theodore Roosevelt and Gifford Pinchot, turned away from Powell's decentralist vision to embrace an ideal of federalized resource ownership and management. Not until the 1950s would a biography of Powell appear, and even now we have not quite grasped or sought to implement his essential vision of adaptive institutions.

I am not, in reviewing these events, calling for a radically "new history" of the American West, but rather for a history that goes back to and builds on Powell's early insights into the significance of the land for the region and the need for social adaptation. It is a history that, after Powell's death in 1902, evolves through the work of such figures as Walter Prescott Webb, James Malin, and Wallace Stegner. It is also a history that visualizes the land through the help of scientists who have followed in the wake of Powell—geologists, ecologists, climatologists, and the like—yet also sees the land through the eyes of the region's writers and painters, portraying it in private and personal as well as public and objective terms. It is a history that centers on a continuing conflict over natural resources, on land speculation, on water development, on mining leases, on agriculture as an adaptive process, on the recruitment of a rural and urban population, on cultural differences among the various peoples contending for possession. None of that is really new as a syllabus for western history, but all of it needs to be regularly updated and expanded by each generation.

What is new, and could never have been anticipated by Powell, who like others of his time was convinced of the general upward trend of history, is our modern experience with environmental destruction. More than a century after he went down the pristine Colorado, we understand that we have made the river, as we have made the West, over into a very different entity. The new Colorado, dammed many times, may be better as an engine of wealth and comfort, but it is not better as a river. It is more laden with salt and less able to support its former ecosystems. A similar decline has taken place in environments all over the West. The air is more polluted, the soil is more depleted and eroded, the fauna is considerably more impoverished than it was at the time of the Civil War. These are all measurable changes, and by almost universal consent they are downward changes in environmental quality. Some observers, it is true, may not acknowledge them as *significant* declines when compared to the region's economic growth figures, but even the boosters generally admit that the brown air hanging over Salt Lake City on a winter's day is not as good as the air that Brigham Young once breathed.

The history we write of the western land today must inevitably reflect a more critical attitude toward progress and of the westward movement that was its geographical correlate. How critical an attitude is a matter of individual judgment. But a western history completely devoid of environmental criticism is intellectually as well as morally bankrupt, or it is an expression of colossal innocence.

The history of the West we write in the future must also help us understand how and why that degradation of the environment has occurred. The leading reasons are many: We can blame population increase, economic culture, government policy, ethnic traditions, community instability, international wars and other events, or the modern technology of mobility and industrialism. Which of those reasons best explains why so much of the West, from Hanford to Rocky Flats, has become radioactive? Which can best explain why, in the next century, the West may experience a long-term desiccation due to a global greenhouse effect caused by the burning of fossil fuels? Why did a people who were so manifestly in awe of the western landscape manage to strip away most of its minerals, leaving behind so much devastation? Uncovering the wellsprings of those environmental changes will take us far beyond Powell, beyond the issues of agricultural adaptation, and into the deeper, hidden recesses of the American and human imagination.

My ambition for western history is to see that full environmental story written. I want to see an environmental history published for each of Powell's hydrographic divisions of the West, ranging from the White River valley of South Dakota all the way to Catalina Island. Even if each has been absorbed into a global market economy, it has special characteristics that have left their traces on local people, settlements, technology, and institutions. I want to read also the environmental history of every group of westerners, from Japanese vegetable growers to Basque sheepherders to polyglot suburbanites, with the hope that we can get a more complete view of what "the land" has meant as lived experience. I would like to see as well a history of every plant and animal species in the region as it has been affected by humans: a history of the black-footed ferret, desert bighorn sheep, sandhill crane, the sequoia, and the Russian thistle. Some of those stories will be about environmental successes—stories of folk who have done a reasonably good job of managing their relations with an ancient, cyclical, and inscrutable nature—while others will be stories of failure and destruction.

A full history of the western land must draw on materials from folklore to serious literature to advanced scientific investigation and government bureaucracies. So far we have not really perfected our strategies for incorporating many of those sources into the field of history. The study of the presence of the land in the folk and popular mind, for example, has hardly begun, at least for the Euro-American immigrants, though we have good ethnohistorical readings of several native cultures. We have very few accounts of the development of environmental expertise, including hydraulic engineers and wildlife biologists, in the West. Even now we have no comprehensive studies of any of the major federal land agencies that hold so much of the region's destiny in their hands. The life and times of the Bureau of Reclamation, to name only one such agency, has never been told from its birth nearly a century ago to its decline and possible demise; nor has that of the Department of Interior.

The debate over the environment has changed radically in the nearly full century since Powell's death, and we will never know just how or whether the Major would have changed with the times. Westerners of many stripes want to lay claim to him because they sense that he shared their interest in, their loyalty toward, the West. He was, in a sense, the father of their country. But today he would be a most bewildered old fellow if he came back to look at the West we have been making: a West that is now the home of 39 million people, including Korean shopowners in Los Angeles, African-American college students in Las Vegas, Montana novelists and poets, Colorado skiers, Kansas buffalo ranchers, and Utah prison guards.[12] How to make a regional whole of all that?

What we still have in common, despite all the demographic, cultural, and ecological changes, is the land and its deep history. Even today, questions about how that land ought to be used, exploited, or preserved continue to dominate western conversations and public policy debates. They also should dominate the work of western historians if they want to be taken seriously. The West continues to create itself with materials furnished by the land, and western history must centrally be the narrative of that creation.

MALCOLM J. ROHRBOUGH

The Continuing Search for the American West: Historians Past, Present, and Future

On the eve of the twenty-first century, what is commonly referred to as the American West stretches forth from the great plains to the highest peaks of the Rockies, across the intermontane plateaus of the Grand Canyon to the varied landscapes of the Pacific Coast. It is a series of physical paradises of infinite variety and shining natural beauty that dazzle the eye and uplift the spirit. The American West has captured the imagination as the essence of the American nation. Its transcendent appeal has reached beyond our borders, and for a hundred years, it has been the destination of tourists from around the world. It is now a focus of images that advertise cigarettes and provide the backdrop to a hundred filmed stories known as "westerns" that are forever inscribed in the texture of our national life. It has become the symbol of the nation's past and present. This American West conjures up images of independence and individual achievement that now seem lost in a series of mass societies characterized by urban decay and sprawling suburbs. It is also, in its way, the nation's future, for it is the center of national changes in the form of growth, heterogeneous peoples, political power, and struggles over natural resources. In short, the problems the nation will confront in the next century are now being played out in the area that we know as the American West.[1]

All of these physical attractions and their attendant images appeal to politicians, sociologists, literary critics, artists, filmmakers, journalists, and others who write about and portray the national experience. For historians, however, the story of the American West is more complicated—or should be more complicated. It involves many different peoples spread across a vast domain the size of much of the continent of Europe; it covers a period of time that includes the Euro-American intrusion into a West older than the American nation itself; it encompasses a variety of changing institutions and influences that have shaped the West and that should be described and analyzed. From historians we expect not a romance but an analysis of the past, a capacity to distinguish between the immediate and the lasting, between the appeal of the physical landscape and the influences and institutions that have shaped the landscape and its peoples. This essay addresses these issues.

In pursing the elusive American West, I consider the First American West and the Second American West. The first part of this chapter describes and analyzes the First American West from the American Revolution to the middle of the nineteenth century, from the Appalachian Mountains to the Great Bend of the Missouri River; the second is from 1850 to the present, from the Missouri to the Pacific Coast. The two are characterized by different landscapes but a common historical past. I will argue that in order to understand the Second American West, it is necessary to consider the historical antecedents of the first American West. Finally, I will discuss the cycles of description and analysis pursued by historians over the past century, with a view to identifying the "new" history of the American West and charting its course for the future.

A preliminary word of caution is in order. The study of the American West offers a departure from the usual interaction of structures and events. Both structures (long-term continuities) and events (short-term changes) must be considered, but on the frontier, structure is not continued but imposed from the outside. So people bring some structures and impose them or they drop others or they invent something new or refashion something old, or combinations thereof, all to fit new circumstances. In the transition from the First to the Second American West, to choose an obvious example, some structural influences vanished and others continued. The change from the First to the Second American West has always dominated the discussions and analyses of the American West. The change was so dramatic—in peoples, institutions, and especially landscape so arresting—that it has filled our mind's eye with images and our historical responses with explanations. It is difficult to separate the structures that made the transition (for example, government, custom, law, religion) and those that were modified (in varied ways) from those discarded. That it is difficult makes it even more important to do so.

The history of the American West begins in the forests of the trans-Appalachian region at the opening of the American Revolution. The time and place are important. The trans-Appalachian region of what would later become Kentucky, Tennessee, and the states of the Old Northwest (such political boundaries are not appropriate in 1775) were the first lands west of the mountains settled by Euro-American families from what we generally call the English colonies. It was here, in several varying forms and different ways, that the shape and character of the First American West would be played out in a new place under new rules.

From the first settlements, people in the First American West exhibited two lasting qualities that helped to define them and their places, attributes that would endure over two centuries and across widely varied landscapes. From the beginning, these Euro-Americans questioned and challenged authority. This quality was, in part, a characteristic associated with the American Revolution, which was, after all, a rebellion against the central authority of the British Crown and its local representatives in the colonies. These challenges (often verging on hostility) would later expand to include a continuing antagonism against federal, state, territorial, and even local government. In its purest form, its practitioners would constitute themselves a sovereign authority and assume the powers of government as the occasion demanded. From the claims clubs of the Middle West in the 1830s and 1840s to the miners' camp meetings of the 1850s and 1860s, this popular assumption of sovereignty became deeply rooted in the American West.[2] Second, these people exhibited an uncontrolled and continuing desire to seize and exploit natural resources. These resources ranged from land for cultivation, town sites, salt springs, and mill sites in the nineteenth century to timber reserves, oil leases, and shopping malls in the twentieth. These acquisitive instincts were found in both individuals and groups organized in pursuit of the same ends.

The First American West began at noon on a day in April 1775 in a copse at the junction of two small streams in what was known to Euro-Americans as the Kentucky Country. On this occasion, a group of entrepreneurs and settlers (whose objectives were the same) began clearing the land to construct a palisaded blockhouse to symbolize their intention to remain in this country. It was a coincidence that the clearing of the land in that place west of the mountains in defiance of central authority coincided with momentous events at Lexington and Concord that would mark a political demarcation line and create a new nation. For the participants, this activity in the clearing was surely just another exercise in labor for their economic advantage and their physical security. Still, these beginnings signaled that the Euro-American settlement beyond the mountains would go forward in defiance of authority. And, in fact, this initial exercise of construction in the First American West represented a double-edged defiance of authority, for the act simultaneously flouted both the laws of the Crown and those of the colony of Virginia.[3]

It is also noteworthy that this construction exercise in the Kentucky forest was the work of an ambitious entrepreneur. Although laborers in the clearing worked under the direction of a woodsman named Daniel Boone, he was an employee of Judge Richard Henderson, whose large-scale schemes aimed to organize and exploit the Kentucky Country. This brief and distant exercise in pursuit of permanence, therefore, embodied the defiance of authority backed by the intrusion of large-scale (by the standards of the day) economic enterprise. In fact, Henderson laid claim to a vast tract of land (initially as large as the present state of Kentucky) acquired by private treaty with Native Americans, so he was perhaps the first large-scale businessman to seek advantage in the First American West. The roll call of Henderson's entrepreneurial successors would include John Jacob Astor, Charles and William Bent, George Smith, William Randolph Hearst, and Frederick Weyerhauser.[4] For more than two hundred years, the opportunities associated with the resources of the American West would be expanded from town sites and mill sites to mining claims, forests, and water rights.

The pin-pointing of the moment is deceptive, for it simplifies a large-scale Euro-American movement across the mountains toward the interior and focuses this broad movement on a single incident. To spotlight a single moment and one incident does not do justice to the appeal of the lands in the interior of the continent to settler family and speculator alike. And it certainly does not pay suitable attention to the relationship between the land and the original native peoples. These peoples would feel the full force of both qualities associated with the First American West: the Euro-American defiance of authority gradually negated the influence of the state and later the federal government in negotiating with native inhabitants; and the driving determination of various entrepreneurs at many levels sought with unremitting voraciousness the lands of the region uninhibited by any recognized authority of government. And we should note the central role of the Euro-Americans seeking lands in what was then known as the Kentucky Country in defying not only eastern authority but also the rights of native peoples.

The American Revolution that defied the power of the British Empire symbolized for many in the East the assault on central authority by those who wished to exercise more local control, whether in distancing themselves from a Parliament or in setting a tax rate. In the First American West, the rebellion was one against containment and for open access to natural resources west of the Appalachian Mountains. To the extent that eastern authority or Native American power west of the mountains opposed this objective, it could be evaded or crushed.

By the close of the revolution, the Euro-American settlements in the First American West, now substantial in size and spread over several areas, needed to establish their own forms of authority and institutional structures to guard the lands they had settled and to lay the groundwork for continued entrepreneurial activity. The ensuing context involved shaping a society through different ground rules defining authority, the locus of power, and the extent of popular participation in the community. The struggle over the shape of these institutions was short, sharp, and significant. The focal point of the conflict was the Kentucky Constitution of 1792, a document that would define the future shape of the commonwealth and also set a precedent for the new states west of the mountains. The struggle over the constitution again represented rebellion against authority and structural precedent. It was fully expressed in a western context of ideals deemed revolutionary in the years after 1783: that is, the attempt to interpose local sovereignty in place of central authority and traditional prerogative.[5]

In the Kentucky of 1792 (the term is now appropriate, for it defined a Virginia county laid off west of the mountains in autumn 1776), the heirs of such rebellious act proposed to reduce the authority of government institutions so as to make economic and political opportunities more available to all citizens. The means to this end was a constitution that provided for the abolition of slavery, for taxation on uncultivated lands (which threatened the emerging planter class and speculators), for a unicameral legislature, and for free suffrage by ballot (as opposed to viva-voce voting), including the vote for women. Equally important to the principle of renegotiating authority was a new judicial system proposed by the so-called radicals, which called for simplified procedures in law and courts and deliberately ignored the English common law with its regard for precedent and circumvented the lawyers who were necessary to such a system. It proposed, instead, a new code of law that opened the court system to all citizens of the state. In the end, this attempt to invest the First American West with a new kind of authority lost in a close vote at the Kentucky Constitutional Convention. That the effort failed does not make its ideas any less remarkable. The constitution that emerged privileged stability and precedent by establishing rules through which the state's natural resources and lands might be exploited. Nevertheless, the constitutional struggle exemplified the continuing renegotiation of authority and repeated conflicts over the apportioning of political power and natural resources.[6]

Another series of events that helps to shape our understanding of the First American West lies in the failure of Richard Henderson's Transylvania Company. That enterprise failed in both the First American West and in the Continental Congress. We should understand the significance of these two failures. Henderson intended to establish a new proprietary colony, the fourteenth and the first west of the mountains. His failure did not signal a lessening of the entrepreneurial spirit. Quite the contrary, it meant that the opportunities associated with this new place should be divided among many and not reserved for one. The failure also signaled that those who camped on the spot exercised considerable influence in defining the new ground rules applicable to the division of the natural resources in the First American West. Henderson's setback on the economic and political levels was a rejection of the closed pockets of authority represented by a single individual or small group and also for the strong preference of local people for local opportunity shared among many. This attempt of the Euro-Americans to strengthen local sovereignty in mid-continent over the three generations from the close of the American Revolution to the opening of the Civil War reappeared in the form of claims clubs, universal trespassing on the public domain, and innumerable unofficial actions of defiance against the federal government as landlord. In the end, the citizens of the First American West were no more inclined to respect the federal government as landlord than they were to obey the dictates of Richard Henderson.[7]

As the settlers of Kentucky fought over fundamental political and economic principles for the future, the representatives of the thirteen states sought to establish guidelines that would simultaneously serve and control the growing First American West. The results of these deliberations were the Ordinance of 1785 that governed distribution of public lands and the Ordinance of 1787 that laid down a system of government for all the new territories west of the mountains. The first ordinance provided a framework for the distribution of land that through much experimentation and modification endured for two hundred years: from the first surveys of the Seven Ranges in the Northwest Territory to the suspension of the homestead provision in Alaska. The second ordinance provided a structure of government aimed at organizing the territories and effecting an orderly transition to statehood, beginning in the Northwest Territory and eventually extending to the admission of Alaska and Hawaii. Yet even when the debates over government form and operation were ended by statehood, the divisions over the bounty reaped from the public domain continued unabated and sharpened into the late twentieth century and remains vital even now on the eve of the twenty-first.[8]

The ordinances of 1785 and 1787 were designed, among other things, to control those attributes of behavior already perceived as characteristic of the American West. The ordinance on organizing government was meant to hold in check the impulse of Westerners to defy authority—such as dealing individually with Native Americans, evading debts, and ignoring orderly inheritance procedures. And the land ordinance was meant to lay down ground rules for parceling out the great physical resources of the middle of the continent, rules made more generous over the first half century of congressional implementation. Subjected to such restrictions, future entrepreneurial activity would take place within defined limits. The fact that active, energetic, and acquisitive people immediately subverted these ordinances or bent them to advantage suggests that the politics set forth might be evaded but could not be ignored.[9]

At the same time, there developed another trait that characterized the American West from the blue grass of Kentucky to San Francisco Bay; namely, that the West was not so much antigovernment in public deed as in public rhetoric. The contradiction stood. Although vociferous cries appeared against the restrictions imposed on acquisition of the "public domain" and other resources, and endless chorus of pleas arose for assistance from the federal government. This search for federal largess in various forms resembled the search for private capital. Certainly the government represented capital of a kind but from a different source. The resources controlled by the federal government and available for distribution were the property of all the citizens of the Republic. So those resources should have been available to all. The demands for federal resources had a tone of querulous begging that implied entitlement to them and grievance when thwarted. More often than not, the government met such demands with bounties in the form of land, military protection, and subsidies of many kinds. The resources thus flowed in a steady stream over more than a century out to the distant territories and later states of the American West. They continue to flow today.

The experience of the First American West unfolded over three generations in a chaotic mix of differing degrees of continuity and change. The ordinances provided one degree of continuity: They laid down a central authority with delicately balanced guidelines, and they tempered that authority with the increasingly generous provisions of Congress. To these generosities was added the understanding of a political reality in which the federal government would never use coercion against its citizens in enforcing these rules. For example, proclamations urging voluntary compliance (in the case of trespassing on the public lands) replaced the kind of force employed in the Whiskey Rebellion. The large-scale attempts of Euro-American peoples to change the landscape and to create the orderly agricultural world of the late eighteenth and first half of the nineteenth centuries demonstrated another aspect of continuity. The great forests of the First American West disappeared and were replaced by broad cultivated fields. In the South, patterns of staple crop agriculture appeared; in the Midwest, mixed grains and livestock, and in the North, the entrepreneurs' assaults began on the great pine forests of Maine, Wisconsin, and Minnesota.[10]

The First American West was a meeting place of diverse cultures: the Spanish in Florida and the French in Louisiana and the Upper Mississippi Valley intermingled with native peoples and later with the English and the Americans. Euro-Americans and Native Americans met and fashioned new relationships, sometimes for mutual advantage and sometimes for purposes of exploitation. For more than two centuries, these two cultures warily circled one another in postures of cooperation and warfare until the flood of Euro-American settlement and land occupation changed forever the balance of their relationships with Native Americans.[11]

Increasingly, numbers of enslaved African Americans were sent to the outer fringes of the southern frontier to cut and burn, to plant and cultivate, while their white masters and mistresses remained in more settled and healthier places. By the time of the large-scale removal of Native Americans from the South in the 1830s and 1840s, slave labor underwrote the opening of new cotton lands, especially in isolated and unhealthy places such as the Delta counties of Mississippi. The activities of black pioneers have not been studied systematically, yet their work in clearing, planting, and building was central to the Euro-American expansion in the South that began in the 1740s.[12]

The uniformity of land forms and settlement patterns observed in the First American West was broken dramatically just before mid-nineteenth century by the advance of Euro-Americans into the Second American West. The term "American West" can be misleading because it refers mainly to the American experience, not to that of Native Americans and Hispanic peoples and African Americans, who had long shared the region. Representatives of the Spanish Empire established Santa Fe in 1610, an imperial step that paralleled the planting of the first English colony at Jamestown. The image of Coronado lost in a sea of grass on what we refer to as the Great Plains is a vivid reminder of the Spanish presence amid spacious distances. The new characteristics of the Second American West were vast panoramas, dramatic new land forms, and changes in flora and fauna. The visual sense of "new" was amply attested to by the accounts of the first Euro-Americans who encountered it. Descriptions of "the

Great American Desert," mountains that touched the sky, great canyons as deep as the mountains were high, the Edenesque qualities of the future California, and the dense towering forest of the Pacific Northwest all testified to the enormous impact of this landscape on the human imagination. The striking visual images stirred powerful emotions. They conjured up dramatic visions of new beginnings and futures untold; they offered sensually seductive new scenery, opportunities for economic exploitation, and nooks and crannies guaranteed to stimulate intellectual curiosity. In this vision, the Second American West sprang into the human imagination, new but unfinished, and soon the object of creative maneuvering to test the unlimited possibilities for its future.

Yet within this catalog of differences, certain basic structural continuities connected the Second American West to a past. The relentless entrepreneurial drive to exploit natural resources changed in form but not intent. The growing force of nation-building spurred expansion and extended Anglo-Saxon and Protestant cultural values, displacing other peoples in the way. The demands by individuals and groups for federal assistance in these distant enterprises escalated. The power of these historic, generationally repeated goals continued; those who subscribed to them did not pause at the Missouri River or at the line of semi-aridity, or even at the foothills of the Rockies; they pressed energetically toward the mountains and then beyond them. In the Second American West, the focal points of individual and corporate drive for profits expanded to include cattle drives, bonanza wheat farms, and golden minerals, with a new emphasis on the control of scarce, sometimes nonrenewable, natural resources such as forests, water, and oil.

Catching the echo sounded in the First American West, the pioneers, individual and corporate, moved across the rivers and into the plains and the mountains and then issued the familiar cry for help in a venture linked, as earlier, to nation-making. This national ideology, blending expansion with national interest, was not new; rather, it exemplified the way structural continuities, not innovative events, stretched across time and place from the First to the Second American West, from the Appalachians to the Pacific Coast, from the American Revolution to the present. From individual settler families to large corporations, the arguments in support of nation-making blended effectively into the climate of physical expansion and masked selfish interests. The largest group to plead the national interest and seek bounties appropriate to spacious goals was the railroad companies. In their Janus-like pose, even as the railroad builders faced West and drove the gangs of Irish and Chinese laborers who supported their capital investment, they also faced East and pleaded for assistance from Washington. The same hands that drew plans and organized workers to build railroads in one direction were held out in supplication in the other. The federal government responded. The largest "bounties" in the history of the nation were conferred on the railroads to support trans-construction.[13]

This important structural element, the continuity of federal assistance across two hundred years from the First American West of the national road to the Second American West of harbor improvements in San Francisco Bay and later the Central Arizona Project, was strengthened by the constant search for capital and power to initiate and complete the exploitation of natural resources. This abiding influence of capital (generally eastern capital) in undeveloped regions provoked both applause and condemnation. No sooner was capital welcomed as economic benefactor than its influence was bemoaned as resulting in a loss of local control. Although large-scale absentee ownership patterns began with land investment schemes in colonial America and later the First American West, these patterns were repeated in the great distances and wonderful natural resources of the Second American West. In both the First and Second American Wests, capital from New York, Boston, Philadelphia, and Chicago, even London and Paris, was spread across the continent for investment in western railroads, mines, land, and water resources.[14]

In this way, a national ideology formed early and expanded to accommodate later efforts. That ideology—composed of entrepreneurial spirit, national interests, demands for federal assistance, and continuing defiance of authority at all levels but especially federal authority and its offspring, territorial authority, took hold. These intentions to defy or by-pass authority sprang from several influences, some traditional and others more recent. Among the traditional was the continuing sense, refined by argument over years, that the natural resources of the nation, especially its lands, belonged to those who were there. That is to say, these assets were the rightful property of those on the spot or, at the very least, residents of the territory or the state who wished to use resources in pursuit of those magic western qualities of "progress" and "growth." In the Second American West, the resources in dispute included land, timber, water, and minerals, but the grounds for controversy remained the same, namely, national versus local authority.

In the distribution of natural resources, the doctrine of local sovereignty was expanded in the Second American West to encompass mining claims and corporate organization. The enormous wealth generated by mining, wherein the temporary ownership of even a small claim could yield great wealth within a few days or weeks, fueled demands for local sovereignty. The corporate organization of mining that followed, whereby the entrepreneurial capability expanded into ever larger institutional forms, fired these demands. Large corporations developed mines in the most remote areas, and made (and lost) money from a wide range of activities—stock speculation, sale and resale of claims, mining townsite development—that often had little or nothing to do with actually bringing ore to the surface for processing.[15]

A central ingredient in the Second American West's pattern of defiance of authority reflected the actual absence of federal power in remote places at great distances from the heart of national strength. The institutions of government fostered during the First American West under the Ordinance of 1787 remained distant, fragile, and often subject to corruption. Although few territories matched New Mexico for the sheer size and range of corrupt practices, some turned into a series of small rotten boroughs that served the narrow interests of special constituents. The federal and territorial structures of government in the Second American West did not exercise great influence in framing the course of political, economic, or social events. In the generation after the end of the Civil War, the Congress of the United States was not a vehicle for fostering respect for law and federal authority because federal activities too often reflected the power of special interests. The Mining Law of 1872, for example, blatantly offered legalized hunting licenses for individuals (and through them, corporations) to exploit mineral resources everywhere. Laws for land and water in the West displayed a notable absence of civic-minded qualities mixed with a lamentable ignorance about geography and climate. Nevertheless, because Congress drew up legislation on resources, and federal officials interpreted these regulations, the power of Washington came to bear in the most remote areas of the Second American West through laws affecting natural resources.[16]

The Euro-American attitudes toward the different races and cultures that permeated the First American West marched West into almost every community, village, and newspaper editorial in the Second American West. As a result of this structural continuity of attitudes and behavior, the Euro-Americans met the indigenous societies and old cultures of the Second American West head on in conflict. These encounters brought about contact with different kinds of native peoples: nomadic tribes of the plains, subsistence groups of the intermontane plateaus, and powerful and sedentary native peoples of the Pacific Coast. By virtue of prior occupancy, these people already claimed substantial portions of the new continental nation; hence, immediate efforts were begun to undermine their claims in a manner that would not overtly damage the reputation or conscience of the democratic republic. The resulting racial doctrines, therefore, portrayed these native peoples as "barbarous and uncivilized," and in this view the extent of their "uncivilized nature," needless to say, increased in proportion to their physical resistance. The massive defeat of General George Armstrong Custer by Crazy Horse, Sitting Bull, and a united armed force of Native Americans became a national symbol of the rising Euro-American hostility, especially since the battle occurred in 1876 on the eve of the centennial celebration of American independence.[17]

In addition to the historical longevity of Native Americans on the land, the Second American West had substantial numbers of other long-time inhabitants. Euro-Americans also encountered in the Southwest large numbers of Mexican-Americans who had occupied portions of present-day New Mexico since the opening of the seventeenth century and California since the middle of the eighteenth. Moreover, the cultural diversity of the Second American West increased with the systematic importation of Chinese, Japanese, and Filipino laborers in the last half of the nineteenth century. Euro-Americans consistently treated each group as inferior, peoples perceived as foreign and not American. Economic competition with these cultural groups heightened the sense of distance and distaste, from mining claims in mid-nineteenth century to services and agriculture in the early twentieth. Public outcry against "foreigners" led to segregated schools in San Francisco in the early twentieth century, and popular pressure led to the restriction against the Japanese, who were described in the Immigration Law of 1924 as "aliens ineligible to citizenship."[18]

The Euro-American distaste for different cultures viewed as alien and the periodic outbreaks of violence against them sharpened as ideological doctrine begun in the First American West and encoded during the Second American West. During the 1840s, the nationalist doctrine of Manifest Destiny defined what was now considered the "American" mission as one of expansion and included the responsibility to "civilize" the "other" purportedly backward peoples of different cultures, languages, and religions. The new notion of a Manifest Destiny created a powerful sense of national mission geared to establish not another new frontier but a whole continental nation. Around this ideological charge the nation mobilized, creating a moment of national import: the resolve to bring distant points of East and West, formerly involved in contested relations, together in harmonious and purposeful national action. Throughout the hemisphere, into Mexico and Cuba, but especially across the Second American West, these others were defined as peoples who needed to be taught the virtues of American democracy and American economic enterprise by American secular missionaries willing to undertake this cultural reformation. This national mission was favored by a momentous event: the California Gold Rush.

From the opening of the Gold Rush in 1849, some observers argued that Americans rushed to California not only to search for gold but also to carry out a national mission by bringing new lands within a national, democratic, and Protestant orbit. The diary of one forty-niner, for example, spoke with patriotic pride and a sense of mission about his participation in liberating California from the Catholic Mexicans. The role of national ideology now moved hand in hand with concern for the acquisition of wealth. Although California was the site of large gold discoveries, the argonauts of the Gold Rush and their community leaders at home combined the enterprises. During a sermon preached in a Boston church on the eve of the departure of the first ship of argonauts for California, for example, Reverend E. N. Kirk focused not on their search for gold but on their cultural role as civilizers in Roman Catholic and Mexican California. These Bostonian missionaries adopted the pose of rough-and-ready miners, but beneath it, they represented New England standard-bearers of right values. The minister referred not to the cargo of gold-digging machinery and tents on the departing *Edward Everett* but to the sizable library on board that would be donated to the city of San Francisco on its arrival, making proper reading material available for a population in need of religious and moral instruction.[19]

These panoramas of places and peoples in the Second American West immediately challenged the historian for interpretation, now mixed with a confusion concatonation of experiences tied to moving West: the range of peoples, places, events, and variations over time; the difficult questions of continuity and change blended with local issues peculiar to the West, such as the distribution of natural resources, especially water rights, which became national issues by the twentieth century. Suddenly, the agenda of historians directed to description and analysis has become the agenda of national political leaders. Thus, the West is the subject of observers, commentators, journalists, and others who turn to the West to test the national pulse. In so doing, they (along with historians) attempt to analyze a diverse array of heterogeneous historical experiences that include both Native American pueblos and Orange County suburbs, liberal flower children from Haight-Ashbury and libertarian survivalists in the Idaho Primitive Area. Cultural heterogeneity marked both the First and Second American Wests, but it is the significant expansion of cultural heterogeneity that characterizes the Second American West.

The early pioneer families of the First and Second American Wests have always been acutely conscious of their places in history. In the First American West, settlers' organizations and celebratory county histories joined local historical societies and agencies to preserve a heroic catalog of Euro-American triumphs over hostile Native Americans, harsh climates, and primitive beginnings, thus inscribing this history with American origins. In the Second American West, imbued with a continuous fascination with American beginnings, there appeared a new sense of American cultural exclusivity. As early as July 1853, the first American arrivals to California organized "The Sons of the California Pioneers," who were to be divided into two groups: pioneers of the first class, composed of U.S. citizens who arrived prior to January 1, 1849; and pioneers of the second class, those citizens who could document their presence in California prior to January 1, 1850. No foreigners could apply for membership, most especially the Mexicans, even though they had been virtually the only California residents of European cultural heritage prior to January 1848. Almost immediately, interested "pioneers" began to compile lists of eligible persons. The final date for acceptance into California's historical elite was September 9, 1850, the date of that territory's admission to the Union. Historical societies, agencies, organizations of old settlers, and celebratory publications at every level invented and reinvented membership for a nation through patriotic groups, records, and anthems.[20]

At the same time, however, a few voices rendered historical accounts of the Second American West from another perspective. The first, Josiah Royce, took as his text that most dramatic triumph of the early Second American West: namely, the California Gold Rush. Born in the California gold-mining town of Grass Valley, Royce became a professor of philosophy at Harvard. At the age of thirty, he wrote his one-volume history of California, subtitled "A Study of American Character," which covered the years of dominant American participation from 1846 to 1856. The context Royce developed for his story featured rising expansionist sentiments at mid-century, one conscious of significant past achievements (acquisitions, seizures) and future golden prospects; yet a nation also increasingly divided over the institution of slavery and growing religious and cultural intolerance. For Royce, the experiences of immigration, expansion, and wealth were inextricably mixed with the darker hues of moral and economic temptations. And the dilemma was further compounded by the siren song of the California Gold Rush.

For Josiah Royce, the California Gold Rush—American at its most expansive at the moment of ultimate economic opportunity—symbolized the dark side of the American national experience. In his introduction to James W. Marshall's discovery of gold in John Sutter's mill race, Royce wrote, "We are, in fact, now and henceforth to deal with a California that was to be morally and socially tried as no other American community ever has been tried. . . . All our brutal passions were here to have full sweep." And he continued, "Whoever wants merely a eulogistic story of the glories of the pioneer life of California must not look for it in history" where "civilization sometimes seemed to have lapsed into semi-barbarism." Royce cared deeply that American miners expelled Mexicans from legal claims, hung Chileans who did not understand English, and discriminated against the Chinese at every turn. The systematic examination of the exploitative side of the Second American West began with the publication of his history.[21]

This examination of the dark side of American exploration, occupation, and exploitation associated with the Second American West continued. For a century its sobering presence paralleled the sun-drenched meadows and forest scenes offered by Frederick Jackson Turner. But at the close of the nineteenth century, Americans, historians and nonhistorians alike, required—even demanded—Turner's romantic vision in order to celebrate the nation's past as uniquely American and to demonstrate a single national vision during a time of growing divisions in American society. It was the influence of twentieth-century events—war, economic depression, the arrival of different immigrant groups—that led to the wish for a unifying message that could effectively connect an American present and past—hence the appeal of Turner's "thesis."[22]

The thesis soon drew critics and divided the study of the American West itself into Turner thesis advocates and Turner thesis critics. The national unifying theme offered by Turner to the America of 1893 fraught with divisions was seriously challenged in 1931 by the publication of Walter Prescott Webb's *The Great Plains*. Webb's study portrayed the Second American West as an alien country, a territory completely separated from the eastern half of the continent, a place to be studied for its differences not for its similarities to the rest of the nation. From communications (Indian sign language) to firearms (the six-shooter) to transportation (the horse), Webb emphasized difference as experienced on the Great Plains in particular but also, by implication, in the Second American West in general. Webb argued for a new historical paradigm for analyzing the Second American West.[23]

Serious challenges produced by Webb's study changed the dynamics of the debate over Western history. Henceforth, the sides became those associated with the continuity of western history (indelibly and wrongly associated with Turner) and national history; and those historians who focused on the study of the West as regional history, less national in scope. Historians in the latter strain have attempted to provide a degree of theoretical framework based on the idea of a "new West" as regional history.[24]

The study of the American West lagged behind the appearance of new themes and methodologies elsewhere in the profession, but it has rapidly moved to the forefront in the past fifteen years. Historians of the American West have adopted new categories of analysis; namely, gender, race, ethnicity, class, and culture, to which they have added a uniquely western perspective on the environment and its transformation under human habitation. Among a large number of significant works, five examples demonstrate the new themes and methods employed. These include (moving from East to West):

Richard White, *The Middle Ground: Indians, Empires, and Republics in the Great Lakes Region, 1650–1815* (1991), treats the interaction between Euro-Americans and Native Americans in an area centered around the Great Lakes. White analyzes cycles of cooperation and hostility over two hundred years.

John Mack Faragher, *Sugar Creek: Life on the Illinois Prairie* (1986), examines the impact on the land of the arrival of the Euro-Americans and analyzes the growth of a single community over two generations with special attention to gender roles.

William Cronon, *Nature's Metropolis: Chicago and the Great West* (1991), combines the changes in "nature" in the Middle West with the astonishing sweep of Chicago's hinterland. Cronon observes that at its height, the influence of Chicago extended from ranches in Nebraska and Montana to the pine forests of the South.

Paula Petrik, *No Step Backward: Women and Family on the Rocky Mountain Mining Frontier, Helena, Montana, 1865–1900* (1989), describes the world made by a generation of women in a Montana city at the close of the nineteenth century.

Roman A. Gutierrez, *When Jesus Came, the Corn Mothers Went Away: Marriage, Sexuality, and Power in New Mexico, 1500–1846* (1991), examines themes of sexuality and power in the context of cultural interaction over three centuries in the American Southwest.

Together, these new studies analyze the natural world and the interaction of Euro-Americans, Native Americans, and other cultural groups; the creation of new communities of Euro-American settlement and their mixture of cooperation and competition with indigenous populations; the search for economic advantage and its effects on political, social, and cultural spheres over several generations. These five volumes and many other splendid works not cited here represent a new departure in the study of the American West. It is useful to note that three of these examples focus on geographic areas and peoples living east of the Mississippi River, suggesting that the idea of a "new western history" is not confined to one part of the West but instead includes the history of the First and Second American Wests.[25]

A final and, in my view, beneficial new direction is the work of several historians who have described and analyzed the American West in the twentieth century. They have argued that useful categories of analysis, whether gender, race, culture, or natural resources, do not cease abruptly at the turn of the nineteenth into the twentieth centuries. Nor does this date represent a natural demarcation line in these several accounts. These works demonstrate an extended world of large and growing cities juxtaposed against almost empty (and emptying) landscapes; increasingly scarce natural resources, especially water; and incrementally diverse ethnic and racial groups. At the same time, it is important to note that the mixture of continuity and change remains central to the story and categories of analysis remain remarkably similar.[26]

Future opportunities for historians of the American West are limitless. No other field offers such a wide range of peoples, times, places, and cultures. Along with opportunities come challenges. Historians must analyze the dynamics of countless encounters: between the Native Americans and Euro-Americans and their environments; among the Native Americans themselves, and the Native Americans and Euro-Americans; between and among the several cultures that inhabited the First and Second American Wests; the emergence of Euro-American communities in their varied forms at various times. In this final task, we must search to find the strands inherited from the past—in this case from the First American West—separate these out, and mix them with the distinctive new qualities that emerge in the Second American West. The same questions of continuity and change also come to bear in a consideration of the American West in the twentieth century. Within these few guides, historians have the freedom to range across a vast and changing landscape, to cover a thousand years (taking into count the Native Americans and their later interaction with European colonial experiences), and to chose among the experiences of a great diversity of peoples.

We should seize these chances.

GERALD D. NASH

The Global Context of the New Western Historian

During the past decade a group of self-appointed New Western (NW) historians and journalists have made a conscious effort to reevaluate the broad range of Western American history. Such an effort is not surprising since every generation reappraises its past—often providing new perspectives and new interpretations. This continual flow of changing ideas and perspectives is refreshing, for without such a process historical interpretations would be stale and stagnant. Critiques of established orthodoxies should be welcomed. The works of some environmental historians during the 1980s, for example, who challenged the prevailing orthodoxy about the primacy of cultural influences on Western development, provides one example. However, many disciples of the New Western History, who are products of the 1960s, have been busily engaged in belatedly applying New Left perspectives of that era to the history of the American West. In the 1990s members of this now middle-aged cohort have been amplifying some of their youthful 1960s dreams.

The perspectives of the New Western historians are well known; advocates have presented their main themes at dozens of conferences and in the mass media. Although many in the profession granted a quiet and respectful hearing, a growing number of critics gradually began to examine the NW claims. A few of the NW historians even prided themselves on wearing a quasi-uniform: blue T-shirts emblazoned with the slogan Gang of 400. But the wearing of the T-shirts was apparently only an innocent lark, not comparable to Fascist Black Shirts, Nazi Brown Shirts, or the red bandannas of Young Communists.

The claim to "newness" invites closer scrutiny. Major targets of the NW group include Frederick Jackson Turner, who has been dead for sixty years, and his major defender, Ray Allen Billington, who has been deceased for a decade. In setting up straw men and women the NW group blithely ignored the large number of historians writing after 1945 who simply did not accept the Turnerian framework. To name a few, Arthur M. Schlesinger, Sr., John D. Hicks, Paul W. Gates, and George W. Pierson, not to mention Earl Pomeroy, were among those who trained graduate students between 1945 and 1975 who expressly bypassed or rejected the frontier hypothesis. To claim that NW historians were the first to challenge the Turnerian synthesis is to ignore major figures of the previous generation and to make unwarranted claims. Let us maintain historical integrity!

The emergence of the NW group is not an isolated phenomenon; it reflects worldwide trends. Moreover, it is not a phenomenon that is unique to the late twentieth century, but one that has appeared periodically over the years. My main purpose is to explore this broad context rather than serve as a critic. A brief analysis of ideological history in the past provides the necessary background for a fuller understanding of NW history in the present and reveals some common characteristics between the works of ideologically oriented historians in the middle of the nineteenth century and the NW group. By no means does this essay claim that NW historians are necessarily of a totalitarian bent. But it indicates that they share at least some stylistic characteristics with their forerunners. The goal of this essay is not so much to provoke controversy as to provide understanding.

Ideological history—or history as propaganda to reflect current political or social agendas—is not new, of course; it has deep roots in the past. A prominent example was the German historian Heinrich von Treitschke, an ardent advocate of Prussian nationalism and German expansion in the second half of the nineteenth century. A professor of history at the universities of Kiel, Heidelberg, and Berlin (1866–1896), he served also as Prussian state historiographer and edited an influential monthly publication, the *Preussiche Jahrbuecher*. At the same time he dabbled in politics and served in the Reichstag (Parliament), although he had little influence there. But as a publicist and partisan historian his impact was considerable. Like the NW historians, he placed major emphasis on race—to the exclusion of other historical influences. In his case, he stressed the superiority of Germans under Prussian leadership. At the same time he touted the superiority of Germans, he deprecated the influence of Jews, just as NW historians have emphasized the importance of minority groups and castigated the past influence of white Anglo males. Von Treitschke was industrious: He combined his roles as journalist and historian and published a seven-volume work, *The History of Germany in the Nineteenth Century.*[1]

Von Treitschke could not know that his style and method would be developed further by historians who became apologists for National Socialism between 1933 and 1945. Most notorious was Alfred Rosenberg, one of the chief architects of Nazi ideology. A Volksdeutscher born in Estonia, he fled to Germany in 1919, escaping the chaos of post–World War I turmoil in eastern Europe. In that same year he joined the still tiny Nazi Party and became editor of the party's newspaper, the *Volkischer Beobachter* (The People's Observer). It was aimed at the masses, somewhat like *USA Today.* In 1930 Rosenberg published his first book, *The Myth of the Twentieth Century.* Designed to dispel what he considered myths about the past, it won him a place as the party's chief ideologue. In that volume—seeking to challenge what he considered conventional orthodoxy—he laced a prime emphasis on the role of race in history. Like von Treitschke, he championed Germans as a master race and also reflected a virulent hatred of Jews. Rosenberg sought to reevaluate the legacy of nineteenth-century German history and to present a politically correct version of National Socialism, inspired by contemporary social doctrines. Regrettably, scores of German academic historians—Karl Brandi of Goettingen can serve as an example—adopted Rosenberg as a pied piper and followed along on his trail, cheered on especially by the mass media.[2]

Meanwhile, similar processes were at work in Russia. In the Stalinist and post-Stalinist decades many historians labored hard to reflect the official party line. Some of their writings and conclusions sound strikingly similar to what appeared in reference to the American West in the United States in the 1980s. Thus, A. Gromyko wrote in 1957, "However hard the apologists of monopoly capitalism may try to put forward concrete differences between the two bourgeois parties, it is impossible to hide the fact that at bottom they are simply the double face of monopoly capitalism." For a generation Soviet historians busied themselves with rewriting history within a Leninist or Stalinist context. But after 1985 a new generation of revisionists arose seeking to undo their work. As Donald Raleigh noted: "The highly politicized Soviet historical profession responded sluggishly to Mikhail Sergevich Gorbachev's call for reform . . . Soviet historians responded cautiously to the call for change because the profession's intellectual integrity had been destroyed during the Stalin years when historians became [the] creators and defenders of historical myths." In not unfamiliar language A. A. Iskenderov noted in 1988: "In the 'stagnant' years, there flowed from the pens of historians . . . dull works that remained silent about . . . historical truth; they lacked original thoughts and conceptions, and instead of profound analysis . . . they thrust upon the reader ready-made sociological formulas." To which his colleague I. A. Poliakov added in 1988: "We must . . . get away from singular points of view . . . and become accustomed to the presence of diverse views and approaches."[3]

By the 1960s some American historians, admiring the Soviet experience or Marxist ideology, launched what was to become known as New Left history. At the center of their focus was class and race. Within the New Left there were many diverse views and factions, and certainly no single theme characterized the message. Most condemned capitalism and charged it with spawning racism and oppression of minorities and the poor, corrupting culture, and destroying the environment. In condemning much of the American experience in the past, they also ascribed special virtues to the masses of oppressed people (of whom unfortunately there are many in the world), whether the poor, ethnic and racial minorities, or anyone outside the mainstream of a white male–dominated society.[4]

The emergence of the New Left in the United States was not a unique phenomenon but reflected similar trends in Europe and Asia. Historians in the German Democratic Republic, West Germany, Eastern Europe, Maoist China, Japan and southeast Asia came to similar conclusions about America's past. The chorus of critical views came not only from the Left but also increasingly from the Right. In fact, after 1968 the Left and the Right shared many similar assumptions about the United States. As the eminent Czech writer Josef Skoreky recently noted: "Left leaning Americans don't like to hear this, but communists and fascists are two peas in a pod."[5]

That relationship was clearly reflected in the community of German historians during the 1980s, particularly during the controversy known as the Historikerstreit, which was begun by a group of revisionists led by Professor Ernst Nolte of the University of Berlin. Essentially, he and his cohorts argued that the German role in the rise of National Socialism and the Holocaust was not really distinctive or exceptional. Without explicitly excusing these events, they sought to place them within the broader context of European events. The contours of Big Power politics since 1815, a succession of mass killings such as those of the Armenians by the Turks in the World War I era, Stalinist purges in the 1930s, and Russian atrocities during the Second World War were all part of a broader pattern within which Germany was hardly exceptional. Implicitly, revisionists like Andreas Hillgruber, Michael Struermer, and Klaus Hildebrand absolved Germans from special blame for National Socialism and the Holocaust, and they normalized their past behavior. This view suited a new generation of historians, either born or educated after 1945, who were also less burdened with onus than those who had been alive as adult witnesses.

Among the latter, the eminent University of Frankfurt philosopher Juergen Habermas was the most prominent critic of the revisionists. He blamed them directly for distorting the nation's values. "Whoever wants to suppress the blush of shame . . . by resorting to slogans such as 'obsession with guilt,'" he wrote, "whoever wants to summon the Germans back to a conventional form of their national identity, destroys the only reliable basis of our Western loyalty." And Habermas added: "I do not want to ascribe evil intentions to anyone. . . . some of us assume that the work of gaining distance and understanding liberates the power of reflective memory. . . . But others want to use a revisionists narrative to equip a conventional identity with a national history." And in language apropos to Western history, Habermas declared: "Historical interpretations must simultaneously be *political* interpretations in that they support some beliefs about how power works and dismiss others. But they need not be *politicized* interpretations; they need not be weapons forged for a current ideological contest." The dispute raged in the pages of professional journals and newspapers between 1985 and 1988 before it subsided. As in the United States, it reflected not so much a generational conflict but far-reaching ideological differences over history and propaganda.[6]

In a very different cultural climate a similar dispute split the historical profession in Japan. The Japanese government demonstrated a dedication to exculpatory history and a persistent unwillingness to accept responsibility for aggressions and atrocities that occurred five or six decades earlier. Textbooks published in the past fifty years unrepentantly portrayed the Japanese conquest of Korea and the invasion of China in terms so benevolent as to provoke official protests from Seoul and Beijing. Young Japanese were taught to see their country primarily as a victim of American aggression and learned little about the multiple causes of the Pacific war. When the notable historian Saburo Ienaga tried, as he wrote in the preface to the English edition of his thorough work *The Pacific War,* "to show the Japanese people the naked realities," he was subjected to official persecution. Japanese courts upheld the Education Ministry's censorship of Ienaga's factual account of the Rape of Nanking in 1937 and demanded a sanitized version.[7]

The issue came up in a different form during the first half of 1992 when the Japanese prime minister visited Korea and was met by violent protests from some of the 300,000 women whom the Japanese government had forced into prostitution to serve the Japanese army during the Second World War. Since the end of that conflict the Japanese government had consistently denied any involvement. But in March 1992 Professor Yoshiaki Yoshimi went to the Japanese archives and retrieved manuscripts that proved and documented what had been official government policy. And single-handedly he forced the Japanese government to acknowledge its complicity. "I know that Japan only talks about half of its history," said Professor Yoshimi, "the half where Japan is victimized."[8] That could be said as well about some of the interpretations of NW historians.

Although revisionist history has been written at different times and in different cultural milieus, it has some common characteristics. Revisionists have tended to disparage the recent past and to exude a sense of pessimism. Historians writing in this vein have at times been advocates of political or social causes and have viewed their works as tools or weapons to achieve social or political reforms. They focused on race and class as major determinants of human affairs. Theirs was not so much a historical as a social mission. In their ardor they frequently embraced historical determinism and denied free will. Skin color or class created situations from which individuals could not escape. That approach also led to a widespread use of stereotypes, oppressors and oppressed, liberals and conservatives. Related was a romanticization of those who were perceived as victims. This *Weltanschauung* also reflected a strong sense of righteousness and moral superiority. To ward off nonbelievers they charged that they were righting wrongs perpetrated by conspiracies, by predecessors who deliberately avoided writing about the victims. The sense of conspiracy led to what historian Richard Hofstadter once described as a paranoid style. Another common element was intolerance of views other than their own, a we-they syndrome that demanded strict conformity of believers, and suppression or neglect of those whose views were at variance. Historians of this stripe viewed themselves as representatives of the masses, as representing the popular will, even when evidence of a large constituency was lacking. And whatever their cultural background, they tended to reflect a narrow focus, confined either by ideology or national origins. Certainly, other common characteristics between nationalists, Nazis, communists, and New Left historians could readily be identified, but these examples do illustrate some of the more obvious trends.

Negativism is a major characteristic of the NW group. Like the National Socialists who deprecated the Weimar Republic or the Stalinists who condemned Czarists and Trotskyites, some in the NW group chastize the white Anglo males who they allege conquered and despoiled North America. Their perception of Western history is a litany of tragedies and injustices inflicted by the dominant group that imposed its destructive values and institutions on innocent, peaceful, and harmonious societies. Thus, the conquerors ravaged and destroyed Native American civilizations; suppressed, exploited, and displaced Hispanics; and discriminated against blacks; and with their sexist views they kept women in a subordinate position. Few would deny the occurrence of these events. Concern would rather be about the context in which they might be placed by historians. The conquerors also despoiled and ravaged the natural environment, allowing excessive greed to destroy a delicate and precarious ecological balance. It was a bleak indictment in which the critics saw very little that was constructive in the development of the West, only a legacy of conquest. This one-dimensional view was familiar to readers of Herbert Marcuse's *One-Dimensional Man* (1972). It was starkly reflected in an exhibition of nineteenth-century Western art sponsored by the Smithsonian Institution in Washington, D.C., in 1991 where the captions, written in a deconstructionist mode as developed by Paul de Man (the former Nazi), reflected that ideology. That perspective was in stark contrast to the pluralist and pragmatic view of those social critics who argued that "the real world that we inhabit and try to understand and if possible improve is one of people, smart and dumb, ambitious and lazy, good and bad and in between, and institutions, rigid and flexible, free and enclosing, decadent and progressive, as well as the natural environment."[9]

Many in the NW group reflected contemporary popular social and political causes. Like National Socialists, they were preoccupied with race; like Stalinists, with class conflict. Without doubt, race issues have been a major concern of Americans since the 1950s. The preoccupation with class and class conflict came from a neo-Marxist ideological context, implicitly or explicitly. These concerns became increasingly fashionable within a wide range of academic fields in the generation after the 1960s. At the same time the changing role of women in American society also impressed the NW historians. In their effort to be present-minded, they questioned historical detachment or objectivity—always an elusive goal, to be sure.

If the NW historians were especially preoccupied with race, that—in part—was due to the influence of Deconstructionism. The theory was further developed by other avid Nazis such as Paul de Man, a Belgian literary critic who won a considerable following after he came to the United States in the aftermath of World War II. An enthusiastic supporter of Adolph Hitler between 1933 and 1945, de Man was courted and recruited by Yale University in the 1960s where he taught as a revered authority. At Yale he secured a large following and many disciples. Like Alfred Rosenberg, de Man held that objectivity was not attainable and that there were no guiding truths or principles. Like National Socialists, he believed that race was a central theme in human affairs. If Aryans were of superior stock, Jews were an inferior variety that had to be eliminated. In his writings de Man urged his followers to discern hidden meanings of which original authors, artists, or composers were unaware (as was done in the Smithsonian exhibit of Western art). This type of subjectivism—of imputing hidden meanings—became the basis of a highly subjective and emotionally charged form of scholarship. Not all followers of de Man were Nazis, but his theories had very clear totalitarian implications.[10]

The origins of Deconstructionism are found in German philosophical thought. Its grandfather was Martin Heidegger, an avid Nazi in the Hitler era. "The Fuehrer, and he alone, is the sole German reality and law, today and in the future," he proclaimed in 1933.

de Man spent the World War II years writing pro-Hitler and anti-Semitic articles in Belgium for collaborationist newspapers. Before donning the respectability of his Yale professorship de Man called for resistance to "Semitic infiltration of all aspects of European life." Although he did not publicize his Nazi activities after assuming his teaching post at Yale they were hardly an impediment to his great popularity there. Various colleagues became his champions and they published spirited defenses of him even after his Nazi past was laid bare fully. As de Man himself noted: "It is always possible to excuse any guilt because the experience always exists simultaneously. . . . It is never possible to decide which one of the two possibilities is the right one." As *The Nation* observed, de Man was an academic Waldheim. And as Dinesh d'Souza cogently observed: "The opening that [de Man's] theories create for totalitarian ideologies . . . can sometimes accompany, and accentuate, malignant political fanaticism."[11]

Revisionists often sought to create new stereotypes to replace the old.[11] National Socialists had stereotyped the Jews—hooked noses and all—and contrasted them with idyllic Aryan types of Germanic origins. Marxists pilloried exploitative capitalists and plutocrats, contrasting them with noble exemplars of the working classes. In seeking to develop new stereotypes the NW group aimed barbs at historians who were dead, especially Frederick Jackson Turner and Ray Allen Billington, accusing them of distorting Western history. In taking the writings of these men out of the context in which they lived, the critics created straw men and women against whom they could measure themselves, given their emphasis on race, class, and gender. Yet neither Turner nor Billington had large numbers of disciples after their deaths so that an effort to characterize them as representative of historians between 1945 and 1990 was highly inaccurate.

At the same time there was little that was new in the content or interpretation of many New Western historians. Revisionists of Native American history had begun to multiply after 1960; historians of the much-neglected African-American experience surfaced just a few years later. And by 1970 Chicano history was gaining its well-deserved recognition. That was also true of the history of Asians in the West. And some of the most challenging works about women in the region began to appear at the same time. It was simply not true that the NW group was the first to give attention to these subjects—scores of others had preceded them, although they were often not cited.[12]

A romanticization of peoples whom the NW group considered victims was a key feature of their writings. These included the poor, women, and members of racial or ethnic minorities. That white Anglo males were their oppressors was implicit or explicit in such an analysis, just as Jews or capitalists were the villains in Nazi or communist analysis. The emphasis on the masses—on the Volk—was a key element in both communism and National Socialism. In Marxian analysis the focus on the working class and on class warfare is classic. In National Socialism Rosenberg's emphasis on the Volk and on its mythical dimensions was equally classic. It led scores of German historians and social scientists to undertake detailed studies of folk culture and behavior, of villages and small communities. In the United States between 1960 and 1990 many scholars emphasized community studies, tribal traditions, and life-styles of the poor. They also gave special emphasis to the virtues, cultures, social relations, and values of these groups who were presumed to be superior to those of American society in the past.[13] This in no way suggests that Americans who used these perspectives were totalitarian, but merely establishes parallels that may, or may not, be relevant.

A sense of moral superiority also was reflected in some NW writings. That tone was part of a broader social trend perceived by some popular social critics. In commenting on the passing of generations, Neil Howe and William Strauss noted, "The old 1960s one and the emerging 1990s facsimile . . . each . . . has claimed the moral and cultural high ground, casting itself as the apex of civilization and its age-bracket adversaries as soul-dead, progress-blocking philistines. The first time around, the members of that generation attacked their elders; now they're targeting their juniors." And in casting a wide net, one that could perhaps also apply to some historians, they wrote, "Although 1990s-edition Boomers are no throwback to the 1960s, they see themselves as they did then (and always have): as the embodiment of moral wisdom. . . . The idea of telling other people what to do suits them just fine. . . . They simply want to redirect public institutions toward what they consider a socially redemptive purpose."[14]

NW history can be viewed within the broader context of the cultural milieu of the 1980s and 1990s. Such a milieu in part, a recent student of the Holocaust noted, includes rewriting of history combined with a growing mood of moral relativism with "the potential to alter dramatically the way established truth is transmitted from generation to generation." This creates an intellectual climate in which "no fact, no event, and no aspect of history has any fixed meaning or content." Robert Hughes, a perceptive social commentator on the culture of complaint, wrote that the politically correct notion is "that all statements about history are expressions of power; history is only written by the winners and truth is political and unknowable, unless some victim knows it in his or her bones."[15]

Deconstruction provides a context for this approach. As one recent commentator noted, much revisionism reflects "a cultural zeitgeist in which all truth is deemed subjective and all facts are made subject to reevaluation. This state of affairs, so reminiscent of an Orwellian Dystopia, is the world today as it is envisioned by the increasingly influential deconstruction movement." Kakutani goes on to note, "Deconstruction purveys a stylishly nihilist view of the world, which insists that all meaning is relative, that all truth is elusive, and therefore futile. . . . Together with society's current eagerness to blur the lines between fact and fantasy, reality and appearance, the deconstructionists and like-minded thinkers foster a climate in which ideologues and propagandists . . . can try to assail those two pillars of human civilization: memory and truth. . . . The stakes in this battle over history are high." As George Orwell once observed: "Whoever controls the past controls the future. Whoever controls the present controls the past."[16]

In a recent critique of American life historian Arthur Schlesinger, Jr., summarized some prevailing trends. "The invocation of history is indispensable to nations and groups in the process of making themselves," he wrote. "How else can a people establish the legitimacy of its personality, the continuity of its tradition, the correctness of its course?" Often, history has been invoked to justify a ruling class. "The past," wrote British historian J. H. Plumb, "has always been the handmaid of authority." This is "top-dog history, designed to show how noble, virtuous, and inevitable existing power arrangements are. Because it vindicates the status quo and the methods by which power is achieved and maintained, it may be called exculpatory history."

However, historians have also followed in a contrary vein, seeking to justify the supposed victims of power. This is underdog history, "designed to demonstrate what Bertrand Russell called the 'superior virtue of the oppressed' by inventing or exaggerating past glories and purposes. It may be called compensatory history." This kind of history seeks to justify the victims of power, to vindicate those who reject the status quo. Isaiah Berlin wrote most cogently of "the value of a real or imaginary rich historical past to inferiority ridden peoples, for it promises, perhaps, an even more glorious future." Changing interpretations of Western history fall into these categories of historical analysis.

The prime purpose of this essay has been to place New Western history in a historical context. This type of historical writing is neither new nor unusual and reflects striking similarities to other varieties of history, including those of nineteenth-century German nationalists, National Socialists, communists, and New Left interpretations. Such similarities in no way imply that its practitioners are followers of any of these varieties. But these views should be subjected to the same critical analysis as other forms of historical interpretation and should not be accepted uncritically. Like other interpretations, those of NW historians reflect current fashionable ideological trends that, in time, will pass on as another generation develops its own unique perspectives.

Notes

Gressley / Prologue

1. After perusing the massive bibliography of political correctness, one would think that many intellectuals do not consider themselves politically correct unless they have written on PC. The following items, some polemic, some not, are ones that I have found most stimulating: John L. Sullivan, James Pierson, and George Marous, *Political Tolerance and American Democracy* (Chicago, 1982); B. Bruce-Briggs, *The New Class* (New Brunswick, 1979); Alvin Gouldner, *The Future of Intellectuals and the Rise of the New Class* (New York, 1979); Alan Wolfe, ed., *America at Century's End* (Berkeley, 1991); Patricia Aoferheide, ed., *Beyond PC: Towards a Politics of Understanding* (St. Paul, 1992); Dinesh D'Souza, *Illiberal Education: The Politics of Race and Sex on Campus* (New York, 1991); Allan Bloom, *The Closing of the American Mind: How Higher Education Has Failed Democracy and Impoverished the Souls of Today's Students* (New York, 1987); Lynne V. Cheney, *Humanities in America* (Washington, 1988); John Searle, "The Storm over the University" *New York Review of Books* 37 (December 6, 1990), 38-39; Arthur M. Schlesinger, Jr., *The Disuniting of America: Reflections on Multicultural Society* (New York, 1992); Michael Kinsley, "P. C. B. S.," *New Republic* 204 (May 20, 1991), 8; William Phillips, ed., "The Politics of Political Correctness," *Partisan Review* 40 (Fall, 1993), entire issue; Jo-

seph Epstein, "The Academic Zoo: Theory-In Practice," *Hudson Review* 44 (Spring, 1991), 32; John Taylor, "Are You Politically Correct?" *New York Times Magazine*, January 21, 1991, 32–40; Terry Eagleton, *Ideology: An Introduction* (London, 1991); and Roger Kimball, *Tenured Radicals: How Politics Has Corrupted Our Higher Education* (New York, 1990).

2. George Orwell, "Politics and the English Language," in Sonia Orwell and Jan Angus, eds., *The Collected Essays, Journalism and Letters of George Orwell* (New York, 1968,) 4; 127–140.

3. The literature on the cultural wars, matches, and rematches often echoes the PC shouts from the barricades. In addition to those relevant citations in note 1, readers may find provocative, if not informative: James Davison Hunter, *Cultural Wars* (New York, 1991); Gerald Graff, *Professing Literature: An Institutional History* (Chicago, 1987); Henry Louis Gates, Jr. *Loose Canons: Notes on the Cultural Wars* (New York, 1992); Charles Taylor, *Multiculturalism: and "Politics of Recognition"* (Princeton, 1992); Robert Hughes, *Culture of Complaint* (New York, 1993); Andrew Ross, *No Respect: Intellectuals and Popular Culture* (New York, 1989); Darryl J. Gless and Barbara H. Smith, eds., *The Politics of Liberal Education* (Durham, 1992); Jung M. Choi and John W. Murphy, *The Politics and Philosophy of Political Correctness* (Westport, 1992); Karl Galinsky, *Classical and Modern Interactions* (Austin, 1992); and David B. Pankratz, *Multiculturalism and Public Arts Policy* (Westport, 1993); Hilton Kramer, "Old Times & New," *The New Criterion* 12 (February, 1994), 4 9; and Werner Sollors, *Beyond Ethnicity: Consent and Descent in American Culture* (New York, 1986).

4. The new social history has been around long enough to attract a plethora of commentators. A few citations of uneven merit are: Lawrence Veysey, "The New Social History in the Context of American Historical Writing," *Reviews in American History* 7 (March, 1979), 1 12; Thomas Bender, "Wholes and Parts: The Need for Synthesis in American History," *Journal of American History* 73 (June, 1986), 120–136; Geoff Ely, "Some Recent Tendencies in Social History," in George G. Iggers and Harold Parker, eds., *International Handbook of Historical Studies* (Westport, 1979), 55–70; James Henretta, "Social History as Lived and Written," *American Historical Review* 84 (December, 1979), 1293–1322; Robert F. Berkhofer, Jr., "Comment," in *ibid.*, 1326–1330; E. J. Hobsbawm, "From Social History to History of Society," in Felix Gilbert and S. R. Grabaud eds., *Historical Studies Today* (New York, 1973), 261–294; Theodore K. Rabb and R. I. Rothberg, *The New History: The 1980s and Beyond* (Princeton, 1982); and Alice Kessler-Harris, "Social History," in Eric Foner, ed., *The New American History* (Philadelphia, 1990), 163–184.

5. Those select readers who wish to dance with or sit out the New West historians will find much to fill their cards in the bibliographies of the essays that follow.

6. For those readers captivated by thoughts of deconstruction, I would suggest a quick glance at Jacques Derrida, *Dissemination* (Chicago, 1983); Frank Lentriccha, *After the New Criticism* (Chicago, 1980); Jonathan Culler, *On Deconstruction Theory and Criticism After Structuralism* (Ithaca, 1982); Geoffrey Hartman, *Saving the Text: Literature, Derrida, Philosophy* (Baltimore, 1981); and David Lehman, *Signs of the Times* (New York, 1991).

7. Robert Hughes, "Art, Morals and Politics," *New York Review of Books* 39 (April 23, 1991), 21–27.

8. Critiques of the New Western can be found in Sam Howe Verhouek, "Myths Die with Their Boots On," *New York Times*, October 24, 1993, 1E, 5E; William W. Savage, Jr., "The New Western History: Youngest Whore on the Block," *Antiquarian Bookman* 92 (October 4, 1993), 1242 1247; Richard Zoglin, "Back from Boot Hill," *Time* 142 (November 15, 1993), 90–93; Nicholas Lemman, "True West," *Atlantic* 272 (September, 1993), 111–114; and Terence Rafferty, "True West," *New Yorker* 49 (January 10, 1994), 81–83.

9. Recent journalistic forays into the contemporary West chronicling "The New Boom," "Westward Ho," and "The Last Frontier" encompass: Timothy Egan, "Tourists Ride into Town, Cowboys Ride Into Sunset," *New York Times*, July 5, 1992, 1, 4; Bill Turgue, "The War for the West," *Newsweek* 98 (September 30, 1991), 20–35; Gerald F. Seib, "Babbitt's Vision: A Changing West, Changed Politics," *Wall Street Journal*, December 29, 1993, 6; Miriam Horn, "How the West Was Really Won," *US News & World Report* 108 (May 21, 1990), 56–69; and Jordon Bonfante, "Sky's The Limit," *Time* 142 (September 6, 1993), 20–27.

Limerick / The Privileges and Perils of the Western Public Intellectual

1. T. R. Reid, "Shootout in Academia over History of U.S. West: New Generation Confronts Frontier Tradition," *Washington Post*, 10 October 1989.

2. Sandy Shore, Associated Press (Teletype), 12 September 1990.

3. Richard Bernstein, "Among Historians, the Old Frontier Is Turning nastier with Every Revision," *New York Times*, 17 December 1989.

4. Sarah Burke, "The Old West: The New View of Frontier Life," *U.S. News and World Report;* Terry Pristin, "'Taming' of the Wild West Is Rewritten by Scholars: Revisionists Steer away from the 'Heroic Conquest.' They Focus on the Diverse Peoples, Conditions," *Los Angeles*

Times, 14 November 1990; Brad Knickerbocker, "A Century after the West Was 'Won': Historians Reexamine Where the Region Has Been, While Other Experts Debate Where It Is Headed," *Christian Science Monitor,* 18 December 1990; Lewis Beale, "How the West Was Redone: Gunslinging Myths Give Way to New Vision," *Detroit Free Press,* 7 November 1990; Ellen K. Coughlin, "Myth and History Clash As Scholars Question Anew the Traditional Story of the American West," *Chronicle of Higher Education,* 21 November 1990; "Plains Truth: Classic Western Myths Are Unmasked by Today's Scholars," *Elle,* September 1990; Vickie Bane, "Calling *Dances with Wolves* 'Fantasy,' A Historian Sounds a Charge against the Mythic Past of the American West," *People,* 22 April 1991; Richard Bernstein, "Unsettling the Old West: Now Historians Are Bad-Mouthing the American Frontier," *New York Times Magazine,* 18 March 1990.

5. Bernstein, "Among Historians," *New York Times,* 17 December 1989.

6. Unsigned introduction to A. B. Guthrie, Jr., "The Old West Defended—The Real West Defined," *Nieman Reports,* Summer 1990.

7. Larry McMurtry, "Westward Ho Hum: What the New Historians Have Done to the Old West," *New Republic,* 22 October 1990.

8. Larry McMurtry, "Here's HUD in Your Eye," in *In a Narrow Grave: Essays on Texas* (New York: Simon & Schuster, 1968), 3–9.

9. Thomas Kuhn, *The Structure of Scientific Revolutions,* 2d ed. (Chicago: University of Chicago Press, 1970).

10. Frederick Jackson Turner, *The Significance of the Frontier in American History,* ed. Harold P. Simonson (New York: Frederick Ungar Publishing Co., 1963), 32.

11. Ray Allen Billington and Martin Ridge, "The Great Basin Frontier, 1830–1846," in *Westward Expansion: A History of the American Frontier,* 5th ed. (New York: Macmillan Publishing Co., 1982), 474–90; Ray Allen Billington, *America's Frontier Heritage* (New York: Holt, Rinehart & Winston, 1966).

12. Thomas G. Alexander, *Mormonism in Transition: A History of the Latter-day Saints, 1890–1930* (Urbana: University of Illinois Press, 1986).

13. Patricia Nelson Limerick, *The Legacy of Conquest: The Unbroken Past of the American West* (New York: W. W. Norton, 1987).

14. I am in debt to Joseph Porter for calling attention to the absence of the fur trade and to John Findlay for noting the absence of cities.

Thompson / The New Western History: A Critical Analysis

1. Patricia Nelson Limerick, *The Legacy of Conquest: The Unbroken Past of the American West* (New York, 1987) has received the most

attention. See also Limerick, Clyde A. Milner II, and Charles E. Rankin, eds., *Trails: Toward a New Western History* (Lawrence, 1991) for the theory and ideology of the New Western historians. Other key works of this school include Donald Worster, *Rivers of Empire: Water, Aridity, and the Growth of the American West* (New York, 1985), and Richard White, *"It's Your Misfortune and None of My Own": A New History of the American West* (Norman, 1991). This book is an aspect of the broader debate over Eurocentric bias in history that has arisen in recent years and came to public attention during the controversies over the Columbus quincentenary commemorations and the Smithsonian exhibit of frontier/western art. A balanced popular treatment of the New Western History is presented by Ellen K. Coughlin, "Myth and History Clash as Scholars Question Anew the Traditional Story of the American West, *Chronicle of Higher Education,* 21 November 1990, sec. A, pp. 4–6.

2. David M. Wrobel, *The End of American Exceptionalism: Frontier Anxiety from the Old West to the New Deal* (Lawrence, 1993), vii. "One of history's highest goals is to make the past usable," writes Limerick in *Trails,* xii.

3. For a discussion of malaise in western/frontier history, see Roger Nicholas, *American Frontier and Western Issues: A Historiographical Review* (Westport, Conn., 1986), and Gerald Thompson, "Frontier West: Process or Place?" *Journal of the Southwest* 29 (Winter 1987): 364–67.

4. Miriam Horn, "How the West Was Really Won," *U.S. News and World Report,* Vol. 108, 21 May 1990, 56–65; Gerald Kreyche, "Preserving the Myth of the Old West,: *USA Today* (monthly), January 1992, 70–71; Richard Bernstein, "Among Historians, The Old Frontier Is Turning Nastier With Each Revision," *New York Times,* 17 December 1989, and Bernstein, "Unsettling the Old West," *New York Times Magazine,* 18 March 1990, 34–35, 57–59. Richard Andrews, "Fact and Fictionalization of the American West," *Chronicle of Higher Education,* 31 October 1990, sec. B, p. 64, declared that the "myth" of the West faded in the 1960s due to the Vietnam War which proved that the United States could not serve as a "global sheriff." Curiously, Andrews's use of archetypal phrasing, i.e, "global sheriff," might be seen as an unconscious recognition of the myth's pervasive influence and power. Following Andrews's logic, it could be argued that the myth is powerfully reborn in light of the Gulf War of 1991.

5. Ray Allen Billington and Martin Ridge, *Westward Expansion: A History of the American Frontier,* 5th ed. (New York, 1982), viii, declare "the history of the American West is, almost by definition, a triumphal narrative for it traces a virtually unbroken chain of successes in national expansion." See Limerick's harsh critique of Billington in Richard W.

Etulain, ed., *Writing Western History: Essays on Major Western Historians* (Albuquerque, 1991), 277–310.

6. Richard Bernstein, "Unsettling the Old West," 35.

7. Larry McMurtry, "How the West Was Won or Lost," *The New Republic,* 22 October 1990, 32–38.

8. Limerick, *Legacy of Conquest,* 219.

9. Richard Bernstein, "Unsettling the Old West," 34–35.

10. Numerous monographs provide an accurate picture of mining-camp life. A good starting place is Rodman Paul, *Mining Frontiers of the Far West, 1848–1880* (New York, 1963), and William S. Greever, *The Bonanza West: The Story of the Western Mining Rushes, 1848–1900* (Norman, 1972). the uniqueness of women in the nineteenth-century mining communities can be found in the marvelous letters of Louise Clapp, better known by her pen name, Dame Shirley; see Carl I. Wheat, ed., *The Shirley Letters from the California Mines, 1851–1852* (New York, 1949).

11. Clark, in a letter dated September 1, 1959, wrote that anyone who wants to use western materials has "to establish contact with the past, literally . . ." Walter Prescott Webb, "Afterword," *The Ox-Bow Incident* (Signet Classic edition; New York, 1960), 222.

12. This idea is further developed in Gerald D. Nash, "Point of View: One Hundred Years of Western History," *Journal of the West* 32 (January 1993), 3–4.

13. Peggy Pascoe, review of *Gunfighter Nation* in *New York Times Book Review,* 21 March 1993, 20.

14. Rodman W. Paul and Richard W. Etulain, comps., *The Frontier and the American West:* Goldentree Bibliographies in American History (Arlington Heights, Ill., 1977).

15. McMurtry, "How the West Was Won or Lost, 35–36," notes that much of the research breakthroughs claimed by the New Western history movement had been pioneered by other writers decades earlier.

16. Limerick, "Information Overload Is a Prime Factor in Our Culture Wars," *Chronicle of Higher Education,* 29 July 1992, sec. A, p. 32.

17. Donald J. Pisani, "Is There Life After Turner? The Continuing Search for the Grand Synthesis and an Autonomous West: A Review Essay" (review of *Trails*), *New Mexico Historical Review* 67 (July 1992), 291.

18. Martin Ridge, "The Life of an Idea: The Significance of Frederick Jackson Turner's Frontier Thesis," *Montana: The Magazine of Western History* 41 (Winter 1991): 2–13.

19. Donald Worster, "New West, True West: Interpreting the Region's History," *Western Historical Quarterly* 18 (April 1987): 141–56.

20. Comments from a question and answer session on the New Western history, Western Historical Association Annual Meeting, Tacoma, Washington, October, 1990, author's notes.

21. Worster, *Rivers of Empire,* passim. Karl I. Wittfogel, *Oriental Despotism: A Comparative Study of Total Power* (New Haven, 1957), argues that the first truly totalitarian nations came into existence in Asia in preindustrial centuries through control of water resources. There is no criticism of U.S. water policy in the work, and Wittfogel makes a point to warn that Communist states could be as evil as the Nazis due to the nature of totalitarian rule—an analysis very similar to Hannah Arendt's *Origins of Totalitarianism* (new ed.; New York, 1973).

22. Frederick Jackson Turner, "United States History, 1865–1910" *Encyclopedia Britannica,* 29 vols. (London, 1911), 27: 711–35.

23. Norris Hundley, *Water and the West: The Colorado River Compact and the Politics of Water in the West* (Berkeley, 1975) is a far more thoughtful and balanced treatment than *Rivers of Empire.*

24. Worster, "Beyond the Agrarian Myth," *Trails,* 24.

25. Limerick, review of Michael Williams's *Americans and Their Forests,* in *American Historical Review* 96 (October 1991), 1276–77.

26. American Indian Studies sessions, Western Social Science Association, Annual Conference, Denver, April 22–25, 1992. Notes in author's files.

27. Jane Tompkins, "West of Everything," *South Atlantic Quarterly* 86 (Fall 1987), 361, and *West of Everything: The Inner Life of Westerns* (New York, 1992).

28. The works of literary criticism that see the West as representing a feminine region are numerous, but the starting place is always Henry Nash Smith, *Virgin Land: The American West as Symbol and Myth* (Cambridge, Mass., 1950). The New Western historians believe that the old myth of the Frontier West is dangerous and was artificially created by an eastern masculine elite. They urge that a new myth be concocted that will prove more useful to the present. Of course, this view point rejects the possibility that myth is an integral creation of an actual historical process.

29. Fred R. Egloff, "Riding Shotgun," *The Journal* 2 (Spring-Summer 1992), 3, 28; Nash, *Creating the West,* 259–77. In an essay entitled "Unleashing the Western Public Intellectual," Limerick asserts in a few pages that she has dispelled the "mystique of objectivity"; see *Trails,* 66–67. Also, John Mack Faragher, "The Frontier Trail: Rethinking Turner and Reimagining the American West," *American Historical Review,* 98 (February 1993), 106–117. Faragher refers to Gerald Nash's criticism of the New Western historians as "mean-spirited."

30. Nash, *Creating the West: Historical Interpretations, 1890–1990* (Albuquerque, 1991), 276. An eloquent description of the optimistic spirit of the West can be found in his "Where's the West?" *The Historian* 49 (November 1986), 1–9.

31. Kevin Starr, *Americans and the California Dream, 1850–1915* (New York, 1973), viii.

32. Thomas Short and Carol Iannone, "How Politicized Studies Enforce Conformity: Interviews with Julius Lester and Elizabeth Fox-Genovese," *Academic Questions* 5 (Summer 1992), 51. Many of the best recent works on western/frontier history reject the extreme claims and cultivated biases of the New Western historians; for examples, see Sherry L. Smith, "Legend and Ambiguous Truth and the Western Frontier," *Chronicle of Higher Education,* 4 April 1990, sec. B., p. 72, which summarizes her research in *The View From Officers' Row: Army Perceptions of Western Indians* (Tucson, 1990). She writes, "Legend aside, it should be clear that these men [officers] were neither unconscionable exterminationists nor civilization's heroic saviors. Rather, they were complex; contradictory and ambiguous human beings." p. 72.

Abbott / The American West and the Three Urban Revolutions

1. Frederick Jackson Turner, *The Rise of the New West, 1819–1829* (New York: Harper and Brothers, 1906); William H. McNeill, *The Rise of the West: A History of the Human Community* (Chicago: University of Chicago Press, 1963).

2. Patricia Nelson Limerick, *Legacy of Conquest: The Unbroken Past of the American West* (New York: Norton: 1987) and "The Case of Premature Departure: The Trans-Mississippi West and American History Textbooks," *Journal of American History,* 78 (March 1992): 1380–94.

3. Jan De Vries, *European Urbanization, 1500–1800* (Cambridge: Harvard University Press, 1984). A sampling of case studies from different parts of Europe includes Eric Cochrane, *Florence in the Forgotten Centuries, 1527–1800* (Chicago: University of Chicago Press, 1973); Frederic C. Lane, *Venice: A Maritime Republic* (Baltimore: Johns Hopkins University Press, 1973); Susan Karant-Nunn, *Zwickau in Transition, 1500–1547* (Columbus: Ohio State University Press, 1987); Orest Ranum, *Paris in the Age of Absolutism* (New York: John Wiley, 1968).

4. Gideon Sjoberg, *The Preindustrial City, Past and Present* (Glencoe, IL: Free Press, 1960).

5. Janet Abu-Lughod, *Before European Hegemony: The World System, A.D. 1250–1350* (New York: Oxford University Press, 1989); Immanuel Wallerstein, *The Modern World-System,* Vols. 1–3 (New York: Academic Press, 1974–89).

6. Adna F. Weber, *The Growth of Cities in the Nineteenth Century* (New York: Columbia University Press, 1899); Paul Hohenberg and Lynn H. Lees, *The Making of Urban Europe, 1000–1950* (Cambridge: Harvard University Press, 1985); De Vries, *European Urbanization.*

7. *Manchester Guardian,* 17 November 1832 and *Chambers' Edinburgh Journal,* 1858, quoted in Asa Briggs, *Victorian Cities* (New York: Harper and Row, 1965), 52, 83; H. J. Dyos and Michael Wolff, *The Victorian City: Images and Realities* (London: Routledge and Kegan Paul, 1973); Andrew Lees, *Cities Perceived: Urban Society in European and American Thought, 1820–1940* (New York: Columbia University Press, 1985).

8. Eric Hobsbawm, *The Age of Capital: 1848–1875* (New York: Charles Scribner's Sons, 1975); Anthony King, *Urbanism, Colonialism, and the World-Economy: Cultural and Spatial Foundations of the World Urban System* (London: Routledge, 1990).

9. Parker Frisbee, "The Scale and Growth of World Urbanization," in John Walton and Donald E. Carns, eds., *Cities in Change* (Boston: Allyn and Bacon, 1977), 44–58; Kingsley Davis, "The Urbanization of the Human Population," *Scientific American,* 213 (Sept. 1965): 3–15.

10. Brian J.L. Berry and Quentin Gillard, *The Changing Shape of Metropolitan America* (Cambridge, MA: Ballinger, 1977).

11. John Friedman, "The World City Hypothesis," *Development and Change,* 17 (1986): 69–83; Anthony D. King, *Global Cities: Post-Imperialism and the Internationalization of London* (London: Routledge, 1990); Michael Peter Smith and Joe R. Feagin, eds., *The Capitalist City: Global Restructuring and Community Politics* (Oxford: Basil Blackwell, 1987); Saskia Sassen, *The Global City: New York, London, Tokyo* (Princeton, NJ: Princeton University Press, 1991); Max Barlow and Brian Slack, "International Cities: Some Geographical Considerations and a Case Study of Montreal," *Geoforum,* 16 (1985): 333–45.

12. Sam Bass Warner, Jr., "If All the World Were Philadelphia: A Scaffolding for Urban History, 1774–1930," *American Historical Review,* 74 (October 1968): 26–43.

13. Carlos E. Castenada, *Our Catholic Heritage in Texas,* Vol. II: *The Mission Era* (Austin: Van Boeckmann-Jones, 1936); John Reps, *Cities in the American West: A History of Frontier Urban Planning* (Princeton, NJ: Princeton University Press, 1979), 58–71.

14. A recent study in this framework is Thomas D. Hall, *Social Change in the Southwest, 1350–1880* (Lawrence: University Press of Kansas, 1990).

15. John Reps, *The Making of Urban America* (Princeton, NJ: Princeton University Press, 1965) and *Cities in the American West;* Oakah L. Jones, Jr., *Los Paisanos: Spanish Settlers on the Northern Frontier of New Spain* (Norman: University of Oklahoma Press, 1979); Dora Crouch, Daniel J. Garr, and Axel I. Mindigo, *Spanish City Planning in North America* (Cambridge, MA: MIT Press, 1982). For efforts to define cities as settlement types see the following: V. Gordon Childe,

"The Urban Revolution," *Town Planning Review,* 21 (April 1950): 3–17; Mason Hammond, *The City in the Ancient World* (Cambridge, MA: Harvard University Press, 1972); Paul Wheatley, *The Pivot of the Four Quarters: A Preliminary Inquiry in the Origins and Character of the Ancient Chinese City* (Chicago: Aldine, 1971); Robert M. Adams, *The Evolution of Urban Society: Early Mesopotamia and Prehistoric Mexico* (Chicago: Aldine, 1966).

16. The third chapter in Hobsbawm, *Age of Capital,* is titled "The World Unified."

17. David R. Meyer, "Emergence of the American Manufacturing Belt: An Interpretation,: *Journal of Historical Geography,* 9 (1983): 145–74; David Ward, *Cities and Immigrants* (New York: Oxford University Press, 1971); Edward Ullman, "Regional Development and the Geography of Concentration," *Papers and Proceedings of the Regional Science Association,* 4 (1858): 179–98; Jean Gottmann, *Megalopolis: The Urbanized Northeastern Seaboard of the United States* (New York: Twentieth Century Fund, 1961).

18. Roger W. Lotchin, *San Francisco, 1846–1856: From Hamlet to City* (New York: Oxford University Press, 1974); Leonard Pitt, *The Decline of the Californios* (Berkeley: University of California Press, 1966); Albert Camarillo, *Chicanos in a Changing Society: From Mexican Pueblo to American Barrios in Santa Barbara and Southern California* (Cambridge, MA: Harvard University Press, 1979).

19. Rodman W. Paul, *Mining Frontiers of the Far West, 1848–1880* (New York: Holt, Rinehart and Winston, 1963); D. W. Meinig, "American Wests: Preface to a Geographical Introduction," *Annals of the Association of American Geographers,* 62 (June 1972): 159–84.

20. N.S.B. Gras, *An Introduction to Economic History* (New York: Harper and Brothers, 1922); R. D. McKenzie, *The Metropolitan Community* (New York: McGraw-Hill, 1933); Otis D. Duncan, et al., *Metropolis and Region* (Baltimore: Johns Hopkins University Press, 1960).

21. Kenneth W. Wheeler, *To Wear a City's Crown: The Beginnings of Urban Growth in Texas, 1836–1865* (Cambridge, MA: Harvard University Press, 1968); Terry G. Jordan, *German Seed in Texas Soil: Immigrant Farmers in Nineteenth-Century Texas* (Austin: University of Texas Press, 1966); David R. Johnson, "Frugal and Sparing: Interest Groups, Politics and City Building in San Antonio, 1870–1885," in Char Miller and Heywood Sanders, eds., *Urban Texas: Politics and Development* (College Station: Texas A&M University Press, 1990), 33–57.

22. Harold L. Platt, *City Building in the New South: The Growth of Public Services in Houston, Texas, 1830–1915* (Philadelphia: Temple University Press, 1983); Judd Kahn, *Imperial San Francisco* (Lincoln: University of Nebraska Press, 1979); Stephen J. Leonard and Thomas J.

Noel, *Denver: From Mining Camp to Metropolis* (Boulder: University Press of Colorado, 1990); Carl Abbott, *Portland: Planning, Politics and Growth in a Twentieth Century City* (Lincoln: University of Nebraska Press, 1983); Robert Rydell, *All the World's a Fair: Visions of Empire at American International Expositions* (Chicago: University of Chicago Press, 1984).

23. Anthony Sutcliffe, *The Autumn of Central Paris: The Defeat of Town Planning, 1850–1970* (London: Edward Arnold, 1970): William H. Wilson, *The City Beautiful Movement* (Baltimore: Johns Hopkins Press, 1989; Herbert Croly, "Portland, Oregon: The Transformation of the City from an Architectural and Social Viewpoint," *Architectural Record*, 31 (June 1912): 591–607.

24. Norman H. Clark, *Mill Town: A Social History of Everett, Washington, from its Earliest Beginnings on the Shores of Puget Sound to the Tragic and Infamous Event Known as the Everett Massacre* (Seattle: University of Washington Press, 1970); Gene Gressley, *Bankers and Cattlemen* (New York: A. A. Knopf, 1966); Joseph King, *A Mine to Make a Mine: Financing the Colorado Mining Industry, 1859–1902* (College Station: Texas A&M University Press, 1977); James E. Fell, Jr., *Ores to Metals: The Rocky Mountain Smelting Industry* (Lincoln: University of Nebraska Press, 1979).

25. Gunther Barth, *Instant Cities: Urbanization and the Rise of San Francisco and Denver* (New York: Oxford University Press, 1975); Kevin Starr, *Americans and the California Dream, 1850–1915* (New York: Oxford University Press, 1973) and *Inventing the Dream: California Through the Progressive Era* (New York: Oxford University Press, 1985); Chauncy D. Harris, *Salt Lake City: A Regional Capital* (Chicago: University of Chicago Department of Geography, 1940); D. W. Meinig, "The Mormon Culture Region: Strategies and Patterns in the Geography of the American West," *Annals of the Association of American Geographers*, 55 (1965): 191–220.

26. David Landes, *The Unbound Prometheus: Technological Change and Industrial Development in Western Europe from 1750 to the Present* (London: Cambridge University Press, 1969); Alfred D. Chandler, Jr., *Scale and Scope: The Dynamics of Industrial Capitalism* (Cambridge, MA: Belknap Press, 1990); Hohenberg and Lees, *Making of Urban Europe*.

27. Lawrence Goodwyn, *Democratic Promise: The Populist Movement in America* (New York: Oxford University Press, 1976); Melvin Dubofsky, *We Shall Be All: A History of the Industrial Workers of the World* (Chicago: Quadrangle, 1969); John Thompson, *Closing the Frontier: Radical Response in Oklahoma, 1889–1923* (Norman: University of Oklahoma Press, 1986).

28. Shawn Lay, ed., *The Invisible Empire in the West* (Urbana: University of Illinois Press, 1991); Robert Alan Goldberg, *Hooded Empire: The Ku Klux Klan in Colorado* (Urbana: University of Illinois Press, 1981): Kenneth T. Jackson, *The Ku Klux Klan in the Cities* (New York: Oxford University Press, 1967); David Chalmers, *Hooded Americanism* (Garden City, NY: Doubleday, 1965).

29. Summaries of this literature are in Gene M. Gressley, "Colonialism: A Western Complaint," *Pacific Northwest Quarterly*, 54 (January 1963): 1–8, and William G. Robbins, "The 'Plundered Province' Thesis and the Recent Historiography of the American West," *Pacific Historical Review*, 55 (Nov. 1986): 577–97.

30. Roderick D. McKenzie, "The Concept of Dominance and World-Organization," *American Journal of Sociology, 33* (July 1927); 28–42.

31. Roger W. Lotchin, *Fortress California, 1910–1961: From Warfare to Welfare* (New York: Oxford University Press, 1992); Peter Wiley and Robert Gottlieb, *Empires in the Sun: The Rise of the New American West* (New York: Plenum, 1982); Carl Abbott, "The Metropolitan Region: Western Cities in the New Urban Era," in Gerald D. Nash and Richard W. Etulain, eds., *The Twentieth Century West: Historical Interpretations* (Albuquerque: University of New Mexico Press, 1989), 71–98. The national defense economy has supported a new manufacturing base in aerospace and electronics as well as the direct expansion of federal jobs. Regional economists and regional planners have developed a substantial base of information on the spatial concentrations of aircraft production, electronics, and related industries, identifying a California seedbed in Los Angeles and San Jose and ancillary centers in Phoenix, Denver, Colorado Springs, Dallas, Houston, Austin, Portland, and Seattle. See Ann Markusen, Peter Hall, and Amy Glasmeier, *High Tech America: The What, How, Where and Why of the Sunrise Industries* (Boston: Allen and Unwin, 1986).

32. David R. Johnson, et al., *The Politics of San Antonio* (Lincoln: University of Nebraska Press, 1983); David R. Johnson, "The Vicissitudes of Boosterism," in Richard M. Bernard and Bradley Rice, eds., *Sunbelt Cities: Politics and Growth Since World War II* (Austin: University of Texas Press, 1983), 325–54.

33. Joe R. Feagin, *Free Enterprise City: Houston in Political Economic Perspective* (New Brunswick, NJ: Rutgers University Press, 1988); Carl Abbott, "Through Flight to Tokyo: Sunbelt Cities in the New World Economy," in Raymond Mohl and Arnold Hirsch, eds., *Urban Policy in Twentieth Century America* (New Brunswick, NJ: Rutgers University Press, 1992).

34. Joel Garreau, *Edge City: Life on the New Frontier* (New York: Doubleday, 1991); Rob Kling, Spencer Olin, and Mark Poster,

Postsuburban California: The Transformation of Orange County Since World War II (Berkeley: University of California Press, 1991).

35. John Walton, *Western Times and Water Wars: State, Culture, and Rebellion in California* (Berkeley: University of California Press, 1992); Richard White, *Land Use, Environment and Social Change: The Shaping of Island County, Washington* (Seattle: University of Washington Press, 1980); Ed Marston, ed., *Reopening the Western Frontier* (Seattle, Washington: Island Press, 1989).

36. For example, the essays of Barry Lopez and John McPhee and novels by Craig Lesley, Edward Abbey, John Nichols, Ken Kesey, and Ivan Doig.

37. Louise Erdrich, *Love Medicine* (New York: Holt, Rinehart and Winston, 1984); Larry McMurtry, *Texasville* (New York: Simon and Schuster, 1987) and *Some Can Whistle* (New York: Simon and Schuster, 1989).

38. John R. Milton, *The Novel of the American West* (Lincoln: University of Nebraska Press, 1980).

39. In particular, see Harold Innis, *The Fur Trade in Canada: An Introduction to Canadian Economic History*, rev. ed. (New Haven: Yale University Press, 1962); Oscar Handlin, *Boston's Immigrants: A Study in Acculturation*, rev. ed. (Cambridge, MA: Belknap Press, 1979); David M Potter, *People of Plenty: Economic Abundance and the American Character*(Chicago: University of Chicago Press, 1954); and Bernard Bailyn, *Voyagers to the West: A Passage in the Peopling of America on the Eve of the Revolution* (New York: A. A. Knopf, 1986); and Grass, *Introduction to Economic History*.

40. Gene M. Gressley, "The West: Past, Present, and Future," *Western Historical Quarterly*, 17 (Jan. 1986): 23.

41. Walter Prescott Webb, *The Great Plains* (New York: Grosset and Dunlap, 1931); Donald Worster, *Rivers of Empire: Aridity and the Growth of the American West* (New York: Pantheon Books, 1985).

42. Jobs in mining, agriculture, and forestry as a percentage of total employment have been declining since 1910 in Utah and since 1920 in Idaho.

43. Earl Pomeroy, "Toward a Reorientation of Western History: Continuity and Environment," *Mississippi Valley Historical Review*, 41 (March 1955): 579–600; Robert Wiebe, *The Search for Order, 1877–1920* (New York: Hill and Wang, 1967).

44. Gressley, "The West: Past, present, and Future," 5–23; Louis Galambos, "The Emerging Organizational Synthesis in American History," *Business History Review*, 44 (1970): 279–90; Robert D. Cuff, "American Historians and the 'Organizational Factor,'" *Canadian Review of American Studies*, 4 (1973): 19–31; Robert Berkhofer, Jr., "The

Organizational Interpretation of American History: A New Synthesis," *Prospects* (1979): 611–29.

45. John M. Findlay, *Magic Kingdoms* (Berkeley: University of California Press, 1992); Michael Davidson, *The San Francisco Renaissance: Poetics and Community at Mid-Century* (New York: Cambridge University Press, 1989): John Louv, *America II* (New York: Penguin Books, 1983); Robert Venturi, Denise Scott Brown, and Stephen Izenour, *Learning from Las Vegas* (Cambridge, MA: MIT Press, 1972); Rayner Banham, *Los Angeles: The Architecture of the Four Ecologies*(New York: Harper and Row, 1971); Mike Davis, *City of Quartz: Excavating the Future in Los Angeles* (New York: Vintage Books, 1992); Carl Abbott, "Southwestern Cityscapes: Approaches to an American Urban Environment," in Robert Fairbanks and Kathleen Underwood, eds., *Essays on Sunbelt Cities and Recent Urban America* (College Station: Texas A&M University Press, 1990), 59–86.

46. Comparative history of the West has tended to draw on European-dominated resource and settlement frontiers like Canada, South Africa, and Australia. Suggested here are some additional ways in which to structure regional comparisons. See William Turrentine Jackson, "A Brief Message for the Young and/or Ambitious: Comparative Frontiers as a Field for Investigation," *Western Historical Quarterly*, 9 (Jan. 1978): 5–18; Howard Lamar and Leonard Thompson, eds., *The Frontier in History: North America and South Africa Compared* (New Haven: Yale University Press, 1981); Jerome O. Steffen, *Comparative Frontiers: A Proposal for Studying the American West* (Norman: University of Oklahoma Press, 1980); Robin W. Winks, *The Myth of the American Frontier: Its Relevance to America, Canada, and Australia* (Leicester, UK: Leicester University Press, 1971); Howard Lamar, "Comparing Depressions: The Great Plains and Canadian Prairie Experiences, 1929–1941," in Nash and Etulain, *Twentieth Century West*, 175–206.

47. There are also parallels for the period between 1840 and 1890. Southern cities like Memphis and New Orleans shared the commercial ambitions of the age of industry, especially as they looked forward to securing the proposed transcontinental railroad. The work of economic reconstruction after 1865 directly paralleled the development of the West, involving efforts to build a system of railroads and focal cities to integrate the South with the industrial core. There were also political parallels between the "redemption" of southern states in the 1870s and western statehood in the 1870s and 1880s.

48. James N. Gregory, *American Exodus: The Dust Bowl Migration and Okie Culture in California* (New York: Oxford University Press, 1980a).

49. Kevin Phillips, *The Emerging Republican Majority* (New Rochelle, NY: Arlington House, 1969); Kirkpatrick Sale, *Power Shift: The Rise of the Southern Rim and Its Challenge to the Eastern Establishment*(New York: Random House, 1975); Carl Abbott, *The New Urban America: Growth and Politics in Sunbelt Cities* (Chapel Hill: University of North Carolina Press, 1981).

50. Chandler Davidson, ed., *Minority Vote Dilution* (Washington, DC: Howard University Press, 1984); Rufus P. Browning, Dale Rogers Marshall, and David H. Tabb, *Protest Is Not Enough: The Struggle of Blacks and Hispanics for Equality in Urban Politics* (Berkeley: University of California Press, 1984).

51. Richard M. Bernard and Bradley R. Rice, eds., *Sunbelt Cities: Politics and Growth Since World War II* (Austin: University of Texas Press, 1983); Peter Hall and Anne Markusen, *The Rise of the Gunbelt: The Military Remapping of Industrial America* (New York: Oxford University Press, 1991); Abbott, *New Urban America.*

52. D. W. Meinig, *Southwest: Three Peoples in Geographical Change, 1600–1970* (New York: Oxford University Press, 1971).

53. Lawrence A. Herzog, *Where North Meets South: Cities, Space, and Politics on the United States–Mexico Border* (Austin: University of Texas Press, 1990).

54. Wilbur Zelinsky, "The Roving Palate: North America's Ethnic Restaurant Cuisines," *Geoforum,* 16 (1985): 51–72.

55. Walter Prescott Webb, *The Texas Rangers: A Century of Frontier Defense* (Boston: Houghton Mifflin, 1935); David Montejano, *Anglos and Mexicans in the Making of Texas, 1836–1986* (Austin: University of Texas Press, 1987); Paul Fernandez, *The United States–Mexican Border: A Politico-Economic Profile* (Notre Dame, IN: Notre Dame University Press, 1977); Niles Hansen, *The Border Economy: Regional Development in the Southwest* (Austin: University of Texas Press, 1981); Oscar Martinez, *Troublesome Border* (Tucson: University of Arizona Press, 1988); Mario T. Garcia, *Desert Immigrants: The Mexicans of El Paso, 1880–1920* (New Haven, CT: Yale University Press, 1981); Oscar Martinez, *Border Boom Town: Cuidad Juarez Since 1848* (Austin: University of Texas Press, 1978); Ricardo Romo, *East Los Angeles: History of a Barrio* (Austin: University of Texas Press, 1983).

56. William Robbins, "Laying Siege to Western History: The Emergence of New Paradigms," *Reviews in American History, 19* (September 1991): 321–24; Joel Garreau, *The Nine Nations of North America* (Boston: Houghton Mifflin, 1981); Norbert McDonald, *Distant Neighbors: A Comparative History of Seattle and Vancouver* (Lincoln: University of Nebraska Press, 1987); Leonard Eaton, *Gateway Cities and Other Essays* (Iowa City: Iowa State University Press, 1990); Michael A.

Goldberg and John Mercer, *The Myth of the North American City* (Vancouver: University of British Columbia Press, 1986).

57. Lionel Frost, *The New Urban Frontier: Urbanization and City Building in Australasia and the American West* (Kensington, Australia: New South Wales University Press, 1991).

58. Office of Area Development, U.S. Department of Commerce, *Future Development of the San Francisco Bay Area, 1960–2020* (San Francisco, 1959), 34.

59. Francine du Plessix Gray, *Hawaii: The Sugar-Coated Fortress* (New York: Random House, 1972); Edward D. Beechert, *Honolulu: Crossroads of the Pacific* (Columbia: University of South Carolina Press, 1991).

Worster / Rediscovering the West: The Legacy of John Wesley Powell

1. A far more distinguished scholarly work than that popular literature is William Goetzmann's *Exploration and Empire: The Explorer and the Scientist in the Winning of the West* (New York: Knopf, 1966), chap. 15. In his title and in his treatment of Powell as the last in a line of imperialists, however, Goetzmann perpetuates much of the popular romantic thinking.

2. See, for instance, William E. Warne's *The Bureau of Reclamation* (New York: Praeger, 1973), p. 4. "Students of reclamation consider Major Powell the father of irrigation development. . . . The mark of that great conservationist of the nineteenth century was indelibly imprinted on the Reclamation Service." The standard lineage runs from the U.S. Geological Survey, of which Powell was the second and most influential director, to a wide array of other government bureaus. See W. C. Mendenhall, "The United States Geological Survey," *Scientific Monthly*, 36 (February 1933): 117.

3. John Wesley Powell, *Report on the Arid Lands of the United States* (Washington, D.C.: Government Printing Office, 1878), p. 1. This book, according to Samuel Trask Dana and Sally K. Fairfax [*Forest and Range Policy: Its Development in the United States*, 2d ed. (New York: McGraw-Hill Book Co., 1980), p. 39], "contends with [George Perkins] Marsh's work for the distinction of being the most significant document in American conservation history."

4. Powell, *Report on the Arid Lands*, pp. 46–56. Shott's data showed a range of 15 to nearly 28 inches in the subhumid region, of 4 (at Yuma, Arizona) to 20 inches in the arid region, and of 16 to nearly 80 inches in the region of the lower Columbia River.

5. Powell, *Report on the Arid Lands*, p. 41.

6. Select Committee on Irrigation of Arid Lands, *Ceding the Arid Lands to the States and Territories,* 51st Cong., 2d sess., House Report No. 3767 (Washington, D.C.: Government Printing Office, 1891).

7. Ibid., pp. 133–134.

8. Ibid., pp. 133–134.

9. Powell, "Institutions for the Arid Lands," *Century,* XXXIX and XL (March, April, May, 1890).

10. The population statistics come from U.S. Census Office, *Report on Population of the United States at the Eleventh Census: 1890, Part I* (Washington, D.C.: Government Printing Office, 1895). The only other cities in the seventeen-state area that had more than 20,000 people were Galveston, Houston, Dallas, Kansas City, and Omaha. In that year Phoenix had barely 3,000 inhabitants and Albuquerque had less than 6,000 (combining both old and new towns).

11. Thomas G. Alexander criticizes Powell's commonwealth idea as being "highly impractical" because it required far more of a consensus about economic development than existed in the West. See his article, "The Powell Irrigation Survey and the People of the Mountain West," *Journal of the West,* 7 (January 1968): 52.

12. U.S. Bureau of Census, *State and Metropolitan Area Data Book, 1991* (Washington, D.C.: Government Printing Office, 1991), pp. 202–203. The figure of 39 million is based on the Census of 1990 and is an aggregation of the population of the seventeen westernmost states, excluding Alaska and Hawaii. The most populous state is California, with 29.8 million, followed by Texas (17.0), Washington (4.9), Arizona (3.7), and Colorado (3.3).

Rohrbough / The Continuing Search for the American West: Historians Past, Present, and Future

1. Among the many recent articles in popular journals, see, as examples, "The West for the West: Fighting for the Soul of America's Mythic Land," *Newsweek,* Sept. 20, 1991; "A Fight over Liquid Gold," *Time,* July 22, 1991 (cover story on the Colorado River).

2. Allan G. Bogue, *From Prairie to Corn Belt: Farming on the Illinois and Iowa Prairies in the Nineteenth Century* (Chicago, 1963), 31–39; Charles H. Shinn, *Mining Camps: A Study in American Frontier Government* (New York, 1992, reprint of 1885 ed.).

3. For an account of the establishment of Boonesboro, see Malcolm J. Rohrbough, *The Trans-Appalachian Frontier: People, Societies, and Institutions, 1775–1850* (New York, 1978), 21–23.

4. George Smith (1808–1891), the only one of these figures who needs

identification, was one of the largest land speculators in nineteenth-century America. See Alice Smith, *George Smith's Money* (Madison, 1966). His holdings reached hundreds of thousands of acres. He was a British subject whose death duties paid for a British battleship.

5. Gordon S. Wood, *The Radicalism of the American Revolution* (New York, 1992). On changes wrought by the new constitution of the state of Pennsylvania and reactions to them, see Robert Brunhouse, *The Counter-Revolution in Pennsylvania, 1776–1790* (Harrisburg, 1942).

6. Patricia Watlington, *The Partisan Spirit: Kentucky Politics, 1779–1792* (New York, 1972), 209–222.

7. James M. Gaver, "The Boonesborough Experience: Revolution in the 'Dark and Bloody Ground'" (unpublished bachelor's thesis, Princeton University, 1964) analyzes Henderson's planning, preparations, execution, and the reasons for his failure, especially the determination of the prospective settlers not to accept the old relationship between landlord and tenant.

8. Of the voluminous literature on the public domain, note Vernon Carstensen's introduction to *The Public Land* (Madison, 1963); and Paul Wallace Gates, *History of Public Land Law Development* (Washington, D.C., 1970). The most recent historiography of the Northwest Ordinance is analyzed in R. Douglas Hurt, "Historians and the Northwest Ordinance," *Western Historical Quarterly*, 20 (1989).

9. On the evasion of public land law, see Malcolm J. Rohrbough, *The Land Office Business: The Settlement and Administration of American Public Lands, 1789–1837* (New York, 1968), especially chs. 7, 10, 11.

10. On the blend of diversity and continuity, see Malcolm J. Rohrbough, "Diversity and Unity in the Old Northwest, 1790–1850: Several Peoples Fashion a Single Region," in *Pathways to the Old Northwest* (Bloomington, 1981); on the changes in the natural landscape, William Cronon, *Nature's Metropolis* (New York, 1991).

11. Richard White, *The Middle Ground: Indians, Empires, and Republics in the Great Lakes Region, 1650–1815* (New York, 1991); Daniel H. Usner, *Indians, Settlers, and Slaves in a Frontier Exchange Economy: the Lower Mississippi Valley Before 1783* (Chapel Hill, 1992).

12. The literature on this subject for the trans-Appalachian frontier is sparse, but colonial historians have done a number of studies. See, for example, Timothy Silver, *A New Face on the Countryside: Indians, Colonists, and Slaves in the South Atlantic Forests, 1500–1800* (Cambridge, 1990); and Usner, *Indians, Settlers, and Slaves in a Frontier Exchange Economy*. By contrast, Latin Americanists have given much more attention to the subject, e.g., Alida C. Metcalf, *Family and Frontier in Colonial Brazil: Santana de Parnaiba, 1580–1822* (Berkeley, 1992).

13. Robin W. Winks, *Frederick Billings: A Life* (New York, 1991) is an insightful account of the relationship between land grants and railroad financing. About 10 percent of the total land area of the continental United States would be granted to railroads, and the Northern Pacific (Billings' line) received the largest grant, eventually 60 million acres, an area larger by 10,000 square miles than all the New England states (pp. 186–187).

14. On the connection between western resources and eastern capital, see Gene Gressley, *Bankers and Cattlemen* (New York, 1965); Joseph E. King, *A Mine to Make a Mine: Financing the Colorado Mining Industry, 1859–1902* (College Station, 1977); and John Thompson, *Closing the Frontier: Response in Oklahoma, 1889–1923* (Norman, 1986). An excellent overview is Richard White, *"Its Your Misfortune and None of My Own": A New History of the American West* (Norman, 1991). The struggle for control of local resources and their exploitation, especially land rights, became the focus of a political movement in the 1980s known as the Sagebrush Rebellion, whose supporters wished federal lands in the New West returned to the states, where they would be used to support economic development.

15. On the money-making opportunities associated with mining, note Malcolm J. Rohrbough, *Aspen: The History of a Silver Mining Town, 1879–1893* (New York, 1986), ch. 5; on the mix of mining and politics, Michael Malone, *The Battle for Butte: Mining and Politics on the Northern Frontier, 1864–1896* (Seattle, 1981); and on mining and the labor force, David Emmons, *The Butte Irish: Class and Ethnicity in an American Mining Town, 1875–1925* (Urbana, 1989).

16. Howard Roberts Lamar, *Dakota Territory* (New Haven, 1954), analyzes the character of territorial governments in the Second American West. Paul Wallace Gates, *A History of Public Land Law Development,* contains a good discussion of the Mining Law of 1872. That law is still on the books.

17. Evan S. Connell, *Son of the Morning Star* (San Francisco, 1984), has a good account of the reaction to Custer's defeat.

18. White, *"It's Your Misfortune and None of My Own,"* 310–325, 443–448.

19. Edward Payson Abbe, "Journal of a Voyage from Boston to San Francisco, January 28, June 17, 1849," Henry E. Huntington Library, San Marino. A transcript of Reverend Kirk's sermon is found in the *Boston Daily Times,* January 9, 1849.

20. Hubert Howe Bancroft, *History of California,* 7 vols. (San Francisco, 1884–1890), 7:707n.

21. Royce, *History of California; A Study in American Character* (repr. Cambridge, 1896), 221–222. On Royce and California, see Robert

V. Hine, *Josiah Royce: From Grass Valley to Harvard* (Norman, 1992). The sceptical strain of western history received new energy with the publication in 1957 of Earl Pomeroy's important article, "Toward a Reorientation of Western History: Continuity and Environment," *Mississippi Valley Historical Review,* 41 (March 1955): 579–600.

22. Frederick Jackson Turner, "The Significance of the Frontier in American History," in *The Frontier in American History* (repr., New York, 1953), 1–38 is the basic statement.

23. Walter Prescott Webb, *The Great Plains* (New York, 1931). On the creation of the book, see Gregory Tobin, *The Making of a History: Walter Prescott Webb and the Great Plains* (Austin, 1976).

24. Among the many discussions of historians and the New West, I like the analytical approach of William G. Robbins, "Laying Siege to Western History: The Emergence of New Paradigms," *Reviews in American History,* 19 (1991): 313–331; and a quick overview in Alan Brinkley, "The Western Historians: Don't Fence Them In," *New York Times Book Review,* September 20, 1992, p. 1. An insightful attempt to redefine Turner is William Cronon, "Revisiting the Vanishing Frontier: The Legacy of Frederick Jackson Turner," *Western Historical Quarterly,* 18 (1987): 155–176.

25. The choices of these five volumes and the time of fifteen years are both arbitrary. Robbins, "Laying Siege to Western History," is an excellent guide to the recent literature. The self-styled "new western historians," whose work is represented in Patricia Nelson Limerick et al., *Trails: Toward a New Western History* (Lawrence, 1990), continue to ignore the First American West. The urge to start anew in the New West seems to flow, in part, from a frantic determination to find a paradigm to replace Turner's thesis and failing the search, to cut themselves off from anything that could be viewed as remotely Turnerian. Hence, their determination to ignore the Old West in their search for appropriate units of analysis in the "new western history." However dated it might be, Turner's model still lurks in the background, the unseen but omnipresent guest at all invited conferences (however exclusive) on the new western history.

26. Among the historians who deal with the West in the twentieth century, the foremost practitioner is Gerald Nash, whose *American West in the Twentieth Century* (Englewood, Cliffs, 1973) was a pioneering study. Nash has since published several other volumes. On nature and natural resources, see especially the work of Donald Worster, *Under Western Skies: Nature and History in the American West* (New York, 1991). The study of the urban West is well represented by Carl Abbot, *The New Urban America: Growth and Politics in the Sunbelt Cities*(Chapel Hill, 1981).

Nash / The Global Context of the New Western Historian

1. Heinrich von Treitschke, *The History of Germany in the Nineteenth Century,* 7 vols., trans. (New York, 1915–1919); on von Treitschke, see George P. Gooch, *History and Historians in the Nineteenth Century,* 2d ed. (New York, 1946); and Andreas Dorpalen, *Heinrich von Treitschke* (New York, 1957).

2. Robert Cecil, *The Myth of the Master Race: Alfred Rosenberg and Nazi Ideology* (New York, 1972); and Robert Pois (ed.), *Selected Writings of Alfred Rosenberg* (New York, 1970).

3. Donald J. Raleigh (ed.), *Soviet Historians and Perestroika: The First Phase* (Armonk, N.Y., 1983), ix, 244, 250; quote of Gromyko from Max Beloff, "Soviet Historians and American History," in John Keep and Liliana Brisbee (eds.), *Contemporary History in the Soviet Mirror* (New York, 1964), 311. For a survey of Russian historiography, see Cyril E. Black (ed.), *Rewriting Russian History,* 2d ed., rev. (New York, 1962), 3–33.

4. *The New York Times,* July 22, 1992.

5. For a brief summary, see Irwin Unger, "The 'New Left' and American History: Some Recent rends in United States Historiography," *American Historical Review, 72* (July, 1967), 1237–1263.

6. The dispute is discussed in Charles S. Maier, *The Unmasterable Past: History, Holocaust, and German National Identity* (Cambridge, Mass., 1988), and for quotations, 32, 47. Italics added.

7. *The New York Times,* January 27, 1992; July 7, 1992; Arthur Schlesinger, Jr., *The Disuniting of America* (New York, 1992), 50.

8. *The New York Times, January* 27, 1992; and Yoshiaki Yoshimi, "Japan Battles Its Memories," *New York Times,* March 11, 1992.

9. Leonard Silk, "Economic Scene," *New York Times,* May 29, 1992.

10. Dinesh D'Souza, *Illiberal Education: The Politics of Race and Sex on Campus* (New York, 1991), 177, 180, 192.

11. On Deconstruction, see Jonathan Culler, *On Deconstructionism* (Ithaca, 1982); Paul de Man, *Blindness and Insight: Essays in the Rhetoric of Contemporary Criticism* (Minneapolis, 1983); and Jonathan Arac, Wlad Godzich, and Wallace Martin, *The Yale Critics: Deconstruction in America* (Minneapolis, 1983). See also Stanley Fish, *Is There a Text in this Class... The Authority of Interpretive Communities* (Cambridge, 1980), by the self-styled guru of this fad. On Heidegger, see Victor Farias, *Heidegger and Nazism*(Philadelphia, 1989); *The Nation,* January 9, 1988, for essay by Jon Weiner. Geoffrey Hartman, "Blindness and Insight," *New Republic,* March 7, 1988.

12. For extensive bibliographies, see Gerald D. Nash, *Creating the West: Historical Interpretations, 1890–1990* (Albuquerque, 1991), 144–154, 279–300.

13. Alfred Rosenberg, *The Myth of the Twentieth Century* (New York, 1982); and George L. Mosse, *The Crisis of German Ideology* (New York, 1964), for the emphasis on Volk.

14. Neil Howe and William Strauss, "The New Generation Gap," *Atlantic Monthly* 270 (December, 1992), 67, 72.

15. Deborah E. Lipstadt, *Denying the Holocaust: The Growing Assault on Truth and Memory* (New York, 1993), quoted in *The New York Times*, April 30, 1993. Robert Hughes, *Culture of Complaint: The Fraying of America* (New York, 1993); and *The New York Times*, April 30, 1993.

16. Schlesinger, Jr., *Disuniting of America*, 48–49.

Contributors

CARL ABBOTT is Professor and Chair of the Department of Urban Studies and Planning at Portland State University. He is the author of numerous books and articles including, *The New Urban America: Growth and Politics in Sunbelt Cities*, *Colorado: A History of the Centennial State* and *Portland: Planning, Politics and Growth in a Twentieth Century City*. A visiting Professor at many universities, Professor Abbott was Banneker Professor of Urban and Regional Planning at the George Washington University, 1987.

GENE M. GRESSLEY was Director of the American Heritage Center, University of Wyoming, 1956–1988; and All University Professor, 1988–1993. He is the author of *Bankers and Cattlemen*, and *The American West: A Potpourri*, plus a diffuse group of essays. Professor Gressley was President of the Western History Association, 1985.

PATRICIA NELSON LIMERICK is Professor of History at the University of Colorado. She has written the books, *Desert*

Passage: Encounters with American Deserts and *The Legacy of Conquest: The Unbroken Past of the American West* [referred to as the canon of the New Western history], plus a host of articles including serving as a frequent commentator for *USA Today*. Professor Limerick is also a frequent lecturer on the American West from shore to shore and overseas.

GERALD D. NASH is Distinguished Professor of History at the University of New Mexico. He is the author of many books and articles among which are *Perspectives on Administration: The Vistas of History*, *The American West in the 20th Century* and *In Search of the West: Historians Interpretations, 1890–1990*. Professor Nash was President of the Western History Association in 1990. He held the George Bancroft Professorship in American History, 1990–1991, at the University of Göttingen.

MALCOLM J. ROHRBOUGH is a Professor of History at the University of Iowa. He has written numerous books and articles among them, *The Land Office Business: The Settlement and Administration of American Public Lands, 1789–1937*, *The Trans-Appalachian Frontier: People; Societies and Institutions, 1775–1850*; and *Aspen: The History of a Silver Mining Town, 1879–1893*. Professor Rohrbough has held visiting appointments at the Institute for Advanced Study, the Huntington Library and the National Humanities Center.

GERALD THOMPSON is Professor of History at the University of Toledo. He is author of *The Army and the Navajo: The Bosque Redondo Reservation Experiment, 1863–1868*, and *Edward F. Beale and the American West*, plus multifold articles and essays. From 1984 to 1990, Professor Thompson served as editor of the Phi Alpha Theta journal, *The Historian*.

DONALD E. WORSTER is Hall Distinguished Professor of American History at the University of Kansas. He is the author of a plethora of books and articles including *Rivers of Empire:*

Water, Aridity and the Growth of the American West and *The Wealth of Nature*. Professor Worster has held several Fellowships including the Guggenheim, the American Council of Learned Societies, and he was awarded the Bancroft Prize in American History in 1980.

Note on the Artist

Known as the "Artist of the Bighorn Mountains,"
Hans Kleiber (1887–1967), with a sure hand
and the spare lines of drypoint captured
in his etchings the natural grandeur
of his mountain West

Index